Y0-ARL-813

HAVE A NICER DAY

First published in Great Britain in 2009 by Prion
an imprint of the Carlton Publishing Group
20 Mortimer Street
London W1T 3JW

Text and cartoons copyright © 2009 Rickard Fuchs
Design and layout copyright © 2009 Carlton Publishing Group

All rights reserved. This book is sold subject to the condition that it may
not be reproduced, stored in a retrieval system or transmitted in any form
or by any means, electronic, mechanical, photocopying, recording or
otherwise, without the publisher's prior consent.

A catalogue record for this book is available from the British Library

ISBN 978-1-85375-743-3

Printed in the UK by CPI Mackays, Chatham, ME5 8TD

10 9 8 7 6 5 4 3 2 1

HAVE A NICER DAY

61 CERTAIN WAYS
(AND SOME UNCERTAIN ONES)
OF ACHIEVING A BETTER LIFE

Rickard Fuchs

With cartoons by Mikael Fuchs

Translated by Laurie Thompson

PR**I**ON

Contents

INTRODUCTION

We all want to have a better life. Even if we think we have quite a good life, we'd have nothing against it becoming a bit better.

In this book you'll find advice and suggestions for making your life better.

This will include which jobs to avoid, why you should say "and" instead of "but", how to have fun, how not to be impressed when you don't need to be, and what rules apply to life's zebra crossings.

What rumours should you believe in, why shouldn't we harbour grudges, who we ought to mix with, and a very important question: what could life be like?

Most of the advice is serious, even if some of it is wrapped in a soft blanket of humour.

But it's no less serious and important for that!

Some chapters are merely intended to be entertaining – but even in those, you may find a little crumb of truth to latch on to.

SO READ, THINK THINGS OVER – AND ALL THE BEST FOR A HAPPIER AND BETTER LIFE!

LOTTERY TICKETS AND CANDLES

There's a story about an unfortunate, destitute man who bewailed his poverty. Every Saturday, after the National Lottery draw, he would go out into his back garden and appeal to God. "I'm a pauper, God!" he would yell. "I didn't win a penny in the lottery this week. Not even a consolation prize. I won nothing at all."

Every Saturday, without fail, he would appeal to God. "God, I didn't win anything this week either! Not a single penny, God! I never win!" One Saturday, after the draw, he stood there as usual and cried out to the heavens: "God! I won nothing yet again! Why do I never win?!" There was a crash of thunder, then a deep voice boomed down from the skies:

"Give me a chance! Buy a ticket!"

This is a story with a moral.

You can't win the lottery if you don't buy a ticket.

If you don't take part in the race, you can't win. You have to make an attempt if you're going to have a chance of winning. You have no right to complain that things are not turning out as they should if you haven't made any attempt to influence the course of events. There's a wise saying, "It's better to light a candle than to curse the darkness". Buy a lottery ticket and light a candle as well, then you've given yourself a glimmer of a chance.

But make sure you don't set fire to the lottery ticket with the candle.

✳

WHAT COULD IT BE LIKE?

Everything is relative. You can always make comparisons, and you can always ask yourself: what could it be like if only things had turned out differently? Could it all be better? Oh yes, it could nearly always have been better.

"I've just won a million in the lottery. But it could have been two."

"I'm doing pretty well. But I could be doing better."

"Things are going extremely well, but they could be going even better."

You could put it another way and ask: could it be worse? Yes, it could. There's practically nothing that couldn't be worse than it is. Your work could be worse (even lower wages, an even nastier boss), your state of health could be worse, as could the children, your friends, your tooth- ache and the Schwarzenegger DVD you've just rented. (It is rather difficult to imagine how the film could be even worse than it is, but it could be.)

Who is most pleased to have electric light and central heating in his home? The man who's always had such things and takes it for granted, or the bloke who's just moved from a draughty old hovel into a modern flat? The answer is obvious. We're not pleased about things we take for granted. We don't wake up every morning and give thanks for the fact that we have running water in our home. (Especially not if it's running down the walls.) We don't sing a hymn of praise every day because we have central heating but we don't have chilblains. If we did, people would give us some funny looks. But maybe we ought to think now and then about what could have been. It could have been much worse. It's not raining, we're fairly healthy, we weren't born to be child labourers in a brick factory in India and we don't have to take part in karaoke sessions if we don't want to.

It's easier to be contented with your lot if you occasionally think about what it could have been like. If you have a pretty good second-hand Volvo, you don't always have to turn green with envy when you see somebody with a big new Mercedes or a BMW: you can look instead at the people who have a rusty little Honda or an asthmatic old Lada. Or you can take a look at the man riding his moped through the rain. Of course, the thought of what might have been doesn't only apply to material things, it's perhaps even more relevant to the more fundamental aspects of life. Just think if you didn't have any friends. (If in fact you don't have any friends, you can skip the previous sentence.) Imagine what it would be like if you always had to worry about your health, your children, your parents, or your disobedient cat. We hardly ever think about the worries we don't have, because we think we have enough to cope with given the worries we do have.

But we sometimes need to remind ourselves that our life and our world could be very different.

There's an old saying about that: "I used to complain about not having any shoes until I met a man who didn't have any feet."

❂

WATCH OUT FOR NAKED EMPERORS

The world is full of naked emperors. People stand around these emperors, who are not wearing any clothes, and encouraged by the experts, they say: "What lovely clothes the emperor is wearing! Made of gold and silver thread! Oh, they are so beautiful!" The experts point at the naked emperors with their well-manicured fingers and say: "Just look at the beautifully embroidered waistcoat the emperor is wearing! Look at the quality of that silver fabric in his elegant jacket!"

And all the people nod in agreement, saying: "Oh yes, it's so lovely, so lovely!"

If you can see that the emperor is naked, there's no need to pretend he's wearing any clothes. If somebody says about a picture: "There's a deeply contemplative stringency and an atmospheric function in the grey scale that oscillates between incredible expressivity and a marked intention to achieve concentrated simplification" and all you can see is a grey canvas, you have probably met a naked emperor. When a film reviewer writes about a new film by the Bulgarian director Zblkvntzrt (who's been released on licence) that the film is "a quasi-synthesis of scaled-down counterpoint in diminishing disharmony" you know that this is a film about naked emperors and their wardrobes.

It's not only in the fields of art and film that you can come across naked emperors. There are emperors with no clothes in every avenue of life. There are even clothes without clothes. Baggy black garments of poor quality and badly fitting and strangely shaped. But the little label in the collar tells you this is a designer item – and posh. And so people look at the little label and say: "It's lovely! Such an… er… interesting shape and such… er… cloth. Very attractive. And expensive."

There are restaurants that serve naked emperors. It says on the menu: "Sole roulade poached in a white wine sauce and orange marinade with a light dusting of tomatized vegetable julienne and glazed pommes duchesse drenched in extra virgin olive oil with oestrogen-scrambled asparagus butter in a truffle oil parfait."

You are served with a plate containing a small lump of fish and a potato. The head waiter expects you to swoon in sheer delight over this glazed and lightly dusted emperor.

People who have surrounded themselves with a mythical image can also be naked emperors. The myth becomes more powerful than the reality. These people expect to be admired by all and sundry, and to receive special treatment in all contexts. The mythical image tells us that these persons are more remarkable than the rest of us, and we can't see the reality for all the imagined gold threads they have spun around themselves.

Watch out for these naked emperors!

Point them out, just like the little child in the fairy story, and shout: "But he's naked!"

❂

DON'T GROW TOO OLD!

We all want to live for a long time and to be healthy and active. If we can't live for ever, then at least we want to live to be 112, spry and alert to the very end. A famous Italian film director was once asked by an interviewer how he wanted to die. The director replied: "I want to be shot by a jealous husband when I'm 105 years old and he catches me in the act, in bed with his young wife."

Even if we haven't planned quite such a precipitate and violent end for our own lives, the Italian film director's answer reflects some of what most of us want. To grow really old, but still in full possession of all our physical and mental faculties. The end should preferably be nice and cheerful, perhaps with a fireworks display and cheers as the closing accompaniment. Unfortunately that's not what usually happens when you grow really old.

Growing really old generally results in problems. (There are exceptions, of course: 104-year-olds who run the London marathon, dance the tango and have an active sex life, preferably all at the same time. But this is not all that usual.) Most old people have all kinds of pains and difficulties. It's not surprising if you don't hear well, don't see well and don't feel well at the age of 99. You can get pains in your hips and knees, you get palpitations and your false teeth clatter every time you try to eat a bowl of soup. Sometimes your teeth fall into the soup, and then it can be very difficult to find them unless it's a clear broth.

When you're very old your bodily functions can start to fail. Your muscles grow weaker and your reflexes deteriorate. You rarely see 90-year-olds who are outstanding ice hockey players or boxers. Your blood vessels calcify and eventually become harder than your muscles. Your mental capacity can also start to fade as you get older. Your memory is no longer what it never was, and you even forget things you should never remember anyway.

If you're unlucky you spend the autumn of your life in an under-staffed nursing home. There is one nurse per 56 beds. You just lie there, feeling tired, seeing badly, hearing badly, you have pains in your knees and you're somewhat confused. You ring the bell hanging over your bed whenever you are hungry, thirsty, need to go to the toilet or want to ask where you are and who it is screaming in the next bed. Nothing happens. You keep on ringing away until you've forgotten why you're ringing. Then you ask the man in the next bed if it isn't coffee time by now, but the man in the next bed thinks he's a footballer in America and wonders if it's half-time now. You ring the bell again to ask for a cup of coffee, but nobody comes.

You're 98 years of age and you can't even get a cup of coffee.

It's not just your health that can get you down when you're very old. Your family can also get you down. You have children, grandchildren, great-grandchildren and they all think the same thing: isn't the old boy going to die soon? It doesn't matter if you're rich or poor, there's always something for them to inherit. Isn't the old boy going to die soon? Your relatives start having acute shivering fits brought on by greed, and start discussing their inheritance before you're even dead. Discreet, considerate relatives undergo a sort of Jekyll-and-Hyde transformation and are ready to start shouting and fighting over some worthless old painting or a nickel plate carafe. Your cousin's grandchildren, whom you haven't seen for thirty years, suddenly turn up at the nursing home and ask how you are and if you've still got that old gold watch.

"Are you Gerald?" you whisper faintly, trying to guess who this money-hungry youngster is.

"No, no, I'm Brian. Gerald isn't here, he never comes to see you. I'm Brian, I'm here."

"Do you think you could get me a cup of coffee?"

"All in good time. Where's that gold watch? That handsome one with the gold chain?"

There may be advantages in growing very old (although it's not clear what they are), but there are lots of disadvantages as well. They say you get smarter and more experienced as you get older, but there again, somebody once said: "Experience is the comb life gives you when you've lost all your hair."

✺

THE ZEBRA CROSSINGS OF LIFE

When you're going to cross over the road, what's important is not whether the traffic lights are at red or at green, but whether there are any cars coming.

The same thing applies to life.

❇

"OK, my house is ON FIRE. I'll just finish the washing up and then I'll call the fire brigade"

GET YOUR PRIORITIES RIGHT!

We're always having to choose from a variety of options.

What's important, what's less important?

What is quite important? What can we discard, and what do we have to deal with right now? What is considered important or unimportant varies from person to person, of course. People have different priorities, but there are obvious cases of getting it wrong. If your house is on fire, a typical example of getting your priorities wrong would be to think: "OK, my house is on fire. I'll just finish the washing up and then I'll call the fire brigade.".

If you have limited financial resources, you might need to decide your priorities for spending money. "Should I continue to smoke a packet of cigarettes a day, or should I use the money to pay the doctor's fees and ask about why I have such a bad cough? I think I'll buy the cigarettes. No doubt the cough will pass."

This is another obvious example of getting your priorities wrong.

It can sometimes be hard to know what to do. Should you bow to the allure of pleasure, or the call to duty? "We have that big family party on Friday night. But I'd planned to go to the cinema with Meg and see that new tough guy movie starring Arnold Schwarzenegger. They say it's a pretty mean film with lots of action and violence. No doubt the family party will be just the same as usual. I think I'll plump for the family party – there's bound to be lots more fisticuffs, action, fighting and violence there."

There are much more important decisions to face up to than whether to go to a family party or to the cinema. But you still need to ask yourself:

What do I think is important in this life?

This is actually a very serious question and it's not

altogether easy to answer. What do you think is important in this life? Keeping healthy? Having lots of money? Having friends? Children? Your job? Being successful? Being admired? Being famous? Or something entirely different? Working for a better world? Helping your fellow man?

What's important for you can be rubbish for somebody else – but that doesn't matter. The important thing is that you should decide what is important for you.

Once you've decided what is important, you have to give that priority over everything else. There are people (quite a lot of them in fact) who think that their work is the most important thing in their lives. They give priority to work before their family, their children and their friends. These workaholics think that a briefcase packed with urgent papers is more important than their partner or their children. Of course that's OK if you've really thought it through and made a conscious decision to the effect that a big bundle of papers from work is more important (more fun?) than your family. Your job always takes precedence. It may be relevant to wonder if anybody has ever lain on their death-bed and thought: "I really ought to have put in more time at the office."

What you think is important, and hence what you place high on your list of priorities, often changes as time goes by. The classical example, of course, are all those fathers who line up and say: "I spent all my time working when the kids were little, and so I hardly ever saw them. Now that I've had another child, I'll spend a lot more time with him." You might ask yourself whether these fathers had previously devoted any time at all to wondering what their priorities were; or whether they had in fact done so but decided that their work was the most important thing in their life. Perhaps they'd spent hours thinking about it and then concluded that a fancy title (professor, chief cashier, city councillor, drum major) and various status symbols (flared trousers from Armani, ingrowing toenails from Manolo Blahnik, a Rolex watch) were more worthwhile than spending a bit of time playing with a few screeching kids.

But if you've now made up your mind that such things as money and status are the most important things in your life, and hence make them your priorities, is that wrong? Needless to say there are no absolute rights and wrongs in questions like this: everybody has the right to form his or her own opinion. What you really ought to do is to ask yourself: Is this what I really think? And if so, why? Why do I want to make these my priorities? What should I do instead, perhaps?

It's probably advisable to have a cup of coffee, and think it all through one more time.

But there again, should you really choose coffee? Wouldn't tea be better? Or hot chocolate? Decisions, decisions, decisions. You've got to get your priorities right.

❂

HEALTHY HEALTH NAGGING

You naturally lead a better life if you are healthy. And so you should look after your health as best you can. We're overwhelmed with advice on how to live if we want to be healthy, and this advice is sometimes contradictory – as well as changing all the time. One minute it's good for you to eat eggs, but you mustn't put salt on your eggs because salt is very dangerous. And so we're forced to eat our breakfast eggs without salt. Until some new research declares that eggs are extremely bad for you, whereas salt is good. Therefore we can have a boiled egg with salt on for breakfast, as long as we don't eat the egg.

Chocolate is dangerous and bad for you on even dates, but healthy and good for you on odd dates. Strong liquor, which is a sensitive subject, is dangerous, but healthy, but dangerous. In moderate amounts alcohol is good for your heart and your blood vessels if you are getting on in years, but an excess of alcohol is bad for you no matter how old you are. Wine is better than spirits and red wine is better than white wine. Apart from in some research results where spirits are just as good as wine, but worse than spirits. If you drink too much of it.

How much is too much?

Too much is when there's so much that it's not good for you. And how much is that? Too much. Obviously, the recommendations are crystal clear.

We are constantly bombarded with other examples of clear advice on healthy eating. Fatty food is bad for you, unless it's fatty fish, which is good for you. Fatty cheese is bad for you, unless it's feta cheese, which is better for you than spirits. Fatty spirits are worse for you than eggs. Boiled food is better than fried food, always assuming the boiled food isn't fatty and doesn't contain cheese. Unless it's unfatty cheese with no strong liquor in it. Cholesterol is not good unless it's good cholesterol, which is better than bad cholesterol. Eggs should be shelled before eating. Fibre is good for you and reduces the risk of chocolate with salt in. Etc, etc, etc.

It can be a little confusing to try to keep track of what you are supposed to eat, and what is bad for you or even dangerous. You should avoid food that crawls over your plate: it's either alive or well past its use-by date. In either case you shouldn't eat it. As for drinking, water is good for you, as long as it isn't polluted or fluorescent. You shouldn't drink moonshine or turpentine, even if you like the taste of it. It's unhealthy. Coffee that's so strong that it corrodes the cup is not good for you. Nor is it good to drink wine that costs more than £60 a bottle (unless some other idiot is paying for it). If you're paying for it yourself, you may well become badly depressed. It's better to drink beer. It tastes good as well.

It's not only what we eat and drink that affects our health. We should also take exercise, avoid stress, keep out of the sun, be happy and have a good social life. Then we'll be healthy. But the most important thing is that we shouldn't smoke. Life is much better if we don't smoke. Smoking is a sin. It's expensive and it smells bad and it's dangerous. Smoking doesn't only reduce the length of cigarettes, it reduces the length of your life. Smoking is also one of the main causes of statistics, and we all know how dangerous statistics are.

If we follow all the good advice on how to live a healthy life and what we should eat and what we shouldn't eat, we'll be in excellent health when we die.

❂

YOU REAP WHAT YOU SOW

It says in the Bible: "As a man soweth, so shall he reap". That sounds pretty straightforward, but it isn't for some people. However, it does make life easier and more easily understood if you accept that there is a close connection between what you sow and what you reap. If we sow weeds, we can't expect beautiful orchids to grow. We shouldn't be surprised if a lot of grass grows where we've sown grass. But there are people who are disappointed and confounded when peaches don't grow where they've sown parsnips.

There is no 100% connection between what you sow and what you reap. If you're unlucky you can sow the most beautiful flowers, but then the crop fails and you end up with a few small, wrinkled brown stalks. But in most cases, we get roses where we plant roses, and thistles where we sow thistles. The sooner we understand that, the better. For instance, if we sow kindness, happiness or loyalty, we have a pretty good chance of harvesting those things. If on the other hand we sow malevolence, duplicity or envy, we shouldn't be surprised at reaping what we sow.

We can't stand cursing a flower bed where we expected to see beautiful tulips if we only planted nettles there.

It's only nature's justice to give us back what we planted, whether we're thinking about plants or people.

And so we should think about what kind of seed we scatter around us.

❂

BE A BIT NEGATIVE!

Whenever anybody gives advice about how to lead a better or more meaningful life, you're always told: "Be positive!" We're urged to be positive all the time, wherever we turn. Exhortations to be positive rain down on us from all sides. "Be positive!" "Think positive!" "Discriminate positively!"

Of course it's good to be positive and think positive, but it's not always easy. There are occasions in life when everything goes wrong, and you feel irritated and depressed. It's not possible to be positive at such times. It's better to give vent to your irritation, your disappointment and frustration instead of making a desperate attempt to be positive. "I'm having great fun, my house has just burnt down and I've got athlete's foot. It's lucky I got the sack today, and I'm so pleased that I trapped my thumb in a door. All in one day! I feel so terribly positive."

When you're pedalling up the hill of life into a strong headwind, it's almost impossible to feel cheerful and positive. But you have to make the effort, of course, and it could be a good idea to think about what might have been, but sometimes it's good for you to be a bit negative. It's more or less impossible for anybody to be positive the whole time, not even those whose job it is to preach positivism. A good illustration of this is provided by the man who said: "I had intended to buy the book *How to Overcome the Difficulties Life Presents by Being Positive*, but I changed my mind when I heard that the author had hanged himself."

Even in insignificant everyday circumstances it can sometimes be positive to be a bit negative. Perhaps you'd thought of going out to eat one Saturday evening. You think the new five-star French restaurant *Le Grand Colic* would be a good choice. Then you start to think about what it will be like. A haughty and rather snooty *Maître D* will ask you to wait in the bar first. Then, when you've been shown to your table, you'll have to wait for the menu. A supercilious and arrogant waiter takes your order. You have to wait and wait, and when the food finally comes it's not as hot as it should be, nor does it taste very good. You wait for an eternity before the dessert arrives. There's not much of it, and it's much too sweet. After the coffee, which is far too strong for your taste, you get the bill. It's incredibly expensive. All in all, your evening out has been a disaster. So you change your mind and decide to be a bit negative. Instead of eating out that Saturday evening you stay at home and make a gourmet meal for a fraction of what the restaurant would have cost you. No unpleasant *Maître D*, no waiting around to make you annoyed, the food tastes much better and you save money.

Being a bit negative can be a good thing now and then.

❁

HAVE FUN!

That really sounds like a silly piece of advice.

No doubt it is, sometimes. It's not always so easy to try to have fun when you're faced with one problem after another, it's pouring with rain, the roof leaks and you've just won the lottery but lost your ticket. But perhaps that's when you really do need to have a bit of fun. What is the ultimate aim and meaning of life? That's a very good question to which there's no definite answer.

Perhaps the aim and meaning of life is to have fun?

Or it isn't; but there's no reason why you shouldn't have fun even so.

Have you ever asked yourself what you think having fun is? You have to know what you want in order to get what you want. So think for a moment: what do you think is fun? Once you've sorted that out, you can start doing it. (Always assuming that what you happen to think is fun is not against the law, deeply immoral or classified as disorderly conduct.) Try going out of your way to have fun. As we all know life involves more than enough boredom and long johns, and so we have to work a bit in order to make it more amusing. If you think it's fun to throw raw eggs into a fan, go ahead and do that. Maybe not every day, but just at weekends, when you want to let your hair down. If you like fishing, go ahead and do that. It doesn't matter whether the fish are biting or not, the main thing is to have fun. If you think it's fun to play tennis, go to the cinema, blow soap bubbles or drink coffee, go ahead and do that. If you think it's fun to attend funerals (what's the matter with you?), ask yourself if there isn't something else you find fun.

If it's possible for you to have fun at work, make sure that you do so. It may be that not every job is suitable for having fun, but if you work as a clown, for instance, you should be able to have fun at work. If on the other hand you're a funeral director, the chances of having fun are perhaps a little reduced. (You could always try cheering yourself up a bit every time you're about to screw down the coffin lid by asking: "Anything else before we close?")

If you're a lawyer or an estate agent you're sure to be able to have fun at work, without disturbing your clients. After all, most people think lawyers and estate agents are jokers. If you are a doctor you can have lots of fun with your patients until the local health authority catches you at it, and then you'll just have to try to have fun while you're re-training. If you're a member of parliament you can have fun by raising your salary while you raise other peoples' taxes.

Having fun makes you feel good, and so you should do it as often as you can. It's good for you and it's not fattening. (Unless you think it's great fun to eat cream cakes with jam.)

Having fun may not be the only thing in life, but it's rather enjoyable.

❂

AVOID TELEVISION PROGRAMMES ABOUT CROCODILES!

It can be tempting to watch beautiful nature programmes on the television. Many of them are both entertaining and instructive, and hence they can be worthwhile. But one should avoid watching nature programmes abut crocodiles. You can be quite certain that at some point there will be pictures of a flock of antelope coming down to the river bank to drink. Among them there is always a baby antelope looking very similar to Bambi, only more fragile and even sweeter. When this baby antelope dips its head into the river, a seven-metre-long crocodile hurtles out of the water and sinks its serrated teeth into it. The commentator always says something to the effect that "the poor antelope doesn't stand a chance" and we all watch as the cruel, armoured, primeval monster drowns the young antelope, its teeth buried deeply into the baby's neck. Who wants to watch anything like that?! Why do they show things like that? Let's just have nice, cheerful programmes that show us how they make beautiful handbags and smart wallets out of those bloody crocodiles.

❂

JUST AS I PLANNED IT

We like to plan our lives. We write in our diaries what we're
going to do, when we're going to do it, and how we're
going to do it. Then we find out later that it didn't turn
out as we'd thought. Generally speaking things don't turn
out as we planned, even though we've spent a fortune on
a magnificent leather-bound filofax complete with diary,
dates-to-remember lists, pages for things we have to do,
and special yellow don't-forget pages. If things don't turn
out as we'd planned them anyway, there's no reason why
we shouldn't refrain from planning now and then. Be
spontaneous and improvise! Pay no attention to that diary
and the yellow don't-forget pages!

Life gets rather boring if it's too pigeon-holed. We have
to be able to do things without first checking our diaries.
Of course it's possible that things might go wrong if we
improvise, but so what? We can console ourselves with the
thought that they often go wrong even when we try to stick
to our carefully worked-out plans. We can't let our lives be
governed by a diary with notes of what we're supposed to
be doing every minute of the day. Besides, all those notes
can be pretty silly at times. Just how much should we plan
and carefully note down in our leather-bound filofaxes?

"On Saturday I shall be happy. 4 – 7 p.m.."

"Next Wednesday I'll have a Danish pastry with my
coffee. 3.30 p.m.."

"At 2.45 p.m. I shall go to the lavatory."

"In three years I shall divorce Beryl."

You can't plan everything. Things won't turn out as
planned in any case. All kinds of things crop up and
turn our careful plans upside down. The bakery has run
out of Danish pastries when we prepare our coffee next
Wednesday, and Beryl asks for a divorce long before we'd

thought of suggesting it. (She can't put up with all this obsessive planning any longer.) We plan our holidays, walks in the woods and meetings. Why do we attend all these pointless meetings that are unproductive anyway? We plan when we're going to have children, when we're going to get married, when we're going to get a pain in the foot, go to the cinema or die.

What kind of a life is that?

"I shall get married three-and-a-half years from now. I'd better find somebody to marry before then."

No matter how we plan, all the plans will be ruined by unforeseen circumstances. Life is full of unexpected incidents. There'll be traffic jams, torrential rain, strikes or unexpected pregnancies — all those things will make a mess of our plans. It's more fun sometimes at least to take each day as it comes, without having planned anything at all.

Remember the old saying: "The Devil laughs when you make plans."

❂

YOU CAN TEACH AN OLD DOG NEW TRICKS

Who invented all those old proverbs? It's not just that they're often wrong, but they sometimes contradict one another. "There's strength in solitude," one saying tells us, but another maintains the opposite: "United we stand, divided we fall." Well, which is it to be? Shall we stand alone or together? A proverb should be simple, clear and true: "A bird in the hand is worth more than a nail in the foot."

> The more you THINK, the better you feel. Especially if you think of something OTHER than your bad memory.

One of the proverbs that gets it wrong is "You can't teach an old dog new tricks." It suggests that you can't learn anything new, nor change at all, when you get old. But of course you can learn something new and change your opinions after your 25th birthday. Or your 35th. Or your 75th. It's true that your memory gets worse as the years go by, but on the other hand you find it more difficult to concentrate. That means you have to make a bit more effort, which is good for you. Your brain benefits from a bit of effort, no matter how old you are. The more you think, the better you feel. Especially if you think of something other than your bad memory.

It has been proved that even very old people can learn something new. Languages, how to use computers, you can learn anything, even if you're no longer young. It's more difficult, but it's possible.

So, don't be frightened of starting to learn something new!

But what about changing your habits and your opinions when you are older? Is that possible? It's not always so easy to do that; but there again, it's not easy when you're young either! Even very young people (especially very young people!) are usually absolutely certain their opinions are correct. They don't want to change either their opinions or their habits, as any parent will tell you. It's a human characteristic, wanting to stick to what you've always thought and done, irrespective of age. And so that proverb ought really to be: "It's hard to teach old dogs new tricks. And young ones. And middle-aged ones. But it's possible."

❁

THINK FIRST, ACT LATER

Are you the type who goes through life pulling at doors labelled "Push"? And then wondering why the door won't open? So you pull even harder, and still it doesn't open. So you think there must be something wrong with the door.

When things don't turn out the way you thought they would, you might wonder why. Generally speaking, you won't get an answer to that question, and sometimes you will get a reply you don't want to hear. But it's still worth asking, despite that.

Maybe you should have had second thoughts first.

If you have second thoughts first, you often avoid unnecessary mistakes. (People make mistakes even if they have second thoughts first, but then it's due to something else. Having wrong thoughts, for instance. Or not enough thoughts. Or too many thoughts. Or not realizing that the door's locked, in fact.)

There are a lot of famous last lines from people who haven't had second thoughts first.

"We'll be able to make it across the railway line before the train comes."

"I'll just strike this match and then I'll be able to see better into the petrol tank."

"Balancing on that balcony rail is no problem at all."

Even when it's not a life-and-death situation, it can be a good idea to think first and act later. We've all bought something on impulse and then regretted it later.

"Fifty per cent off the sale price for a water-damaged aquarium! I'll take three!"

"What a smashing jacket! Mind you, it's the wrong size and the wrong colour and it doesn't match anything I've got already and it's too expensive really, but it's a smashing jacket. I'll take it!"

Afterwards, you wish you'd had second thoughts.

We act without thinking surprisingly often, even when it's very important. It's bad enough being stuck with a water-damaged aquarium or a jacket we can't wear and can't afford, but it's even worse when we decide to become a sheep farmer or an IT consultant or a poet, without a second thought. Cheerfully and impulsively we set out to do something we don't have a clue about, something that can only end up in disaster. And then, when we stand there with our unsheared sheep, our widely reported bankruptcy or our unsold collections of poetry, we think: maybe I should have had second thoughts first.

But there again, what does it say in the next chapter?

When things don't turn out the way you THOUGHT they would, you might wonder why.

✶

ACT FIRST, THINK LATER

Isn't that precisely the opposite to what it said in the previous chapter?

Didn't it say there that you should think first before doing anything? Well, yes; but there are occasions in life when nothing gets done if you don't make the most of an opportunity. If you say to yourself: "hmm, perhaps I ought to, but there again, maybe I shouldn't, but on the other hand…", by the time you've made up your mind the opportunity is likely to have passed you by. Sometimes you have to act quickly or it's too late.

> Elsie is pretty and can fix FREE tickets for Wimbledon — I think I'll marry her. I don't like her all that much, but free tickets for Wimbledon is a big bonus.

There are other reasons why you should act first and think later. Albert Einstein once said that in all the minor and comparatively minor questions you can let your reason hold sway, but that when it comes to the really big questions you should give free rein to your emotions.

Einstein is regarded as an unusually bright lad ($E=mc^2$), so maybe we ought to pay some attention to his advice. When it comes to the really big and important questions (not things like whether or not we should buy a water-damaged aquarium) perhaps we should be guided by our emotions. It's possible we have an inbuilt emotional compass that points us in the right direction when we really feel strongly about something. In those circumstances perhaps we shouldn't have second thoughts first. A good example of an important question like that is who we should marry. Should we rely on our reason or should we leave it to our emotions? Most people will say that we should let our emotions decide, of course. We don't often think: "Elsie is pretty, wealthy and can fix free tickets for Wimbledon — I think I'll marry her. I don't like her all that much, but free tickets for Wimbledon are a big bonus. I'm madly in love with Edna, but so what? Too bad."

On the other hand, Einstein might have been wrong. (Perhaps it should have been $E=m^2c$, and maybe it would be a mistake to marry Edna.)

✻

TAKE NOTICE OF GREEN LIGHTS AS WELL

When you are driving through town you are often forced to stop at a red light. If you come up against two or three sets of traffic lights in a row, each one gleaming with that pretty red colour, you are likely to curse your incredibly bad luck. "Red, red, red – every damned traffic light is at red! It was exactly the same yesterday. The bastards are victimizing me!"

The problem is, we take it for granted that every set of traffic lights will be showing green when we approach. We regard green as normal, whereas red means we are unlucky – especially if we come up against several reds in a row. We don't think there's anything odd or abnormal about passing eight green lights in succession. We regard that as how it should be, nothing to think twice about. And just keep going. But if we were to have the staggeringly bad luck to be clobbered by the unfathomable scheming of the local traffic department and hit a series of eight red lights, we would lose our cool and risk cerebral haemorrhage following an acute attack of high blood pressure. "What's the matter with these damned traffic lights? Have they all got stuck on red?! I'll be late for my dental appointment now. Mind you, why am I in such a hurry to get there? He's intending to drill half my head away."

So we react violently to a series of red lights, one after the other, but not at all if we pass the same number of green lights.

We must learn to take notice of and appreciate the green lights along the way!

It doesn't go without saying that we should always find the traffic lights are at green when we're on our journey. Of course it's a pain and annoying to come up against a series of red lights on our journey, but that's compensated by the fact that sometimes we come to eight green lights in succession. We simply need to take notice of the green lights as well.

If we are colour blind, that changes the situation fundamentally, of course, and we need to do our best to explain that to the police.

IT'LL PROBABLY BE THE OTHER WAY ROUND

Because of some unknown natural law, things hardly ever turn out as you expected them to.

Nobody knows why that is. Sometimes, when you think things are going well, they end up badly. When you know something is going to go badly, somehow it turns out well. You should therefore always assume that things are going to be the the opposite of what you think. The trouble is, if you believe everything is going to be the opposite of what you think, that means you think it will be the other way round and so it will be the opposite of what you thought, i.e. it will be the same as you thought in the first place.

You can try to cover yourself against the fact that things generally turn out to be the opposite of what you had expected. If there are only two possible outcomes, you can assume it will be either alternative A or alternative B. Then you're covered. The remarkable thing is that in situations like that, there always turns out to be a third way, which was actually impossible and hence you hadn't thought of it. So it's best to assume that everything will be the other way round, without thinking about why or how that will come about. If you always do that, you will never be upset or surprised, and life will be easier. Moreover, everything will turn out just as you expected.

Unless you thought it would be the other way round.

DON'T BE TOO BRAVE

Down the ages, courage has been an admired quality. Being brave has always been seen as a great virtue. Brave war heroes get a medal (even if the medal is often presented posthumously to the next of kin as the courageous war hero died as a result of his bravery).

There is a saying: "There are old divers and there are bold divers, but there are no old bold divers."

Perhaps an excess of bravery is not such a good thing? Where is the borderline between carelessness and courage? When is bravery not bravery at all, but stupidity? If a lone soldier takes on a whole army, is he astonishingly brave, or incredibly dim-witted?

A fisherman who puts out to sea in a leaky old boat in a raging storm – is he brave? Or imprudent? Or thick?

Can you be clever and far-sighted and brave, all at the same time? Yes, no doubt that's possible. But if you can see the dangers in advance and consider those dangers to be unsurmountable and impossible to cope with, is it sensible to expose yourself to them even so? Isn't it better to desist?

It can be wise to be careful about being bold. Or as some sensible (but perhaps not brave) person once said: "It's better to be cowardly for one minute than to be dead for the rest of your life."

❂

WHO SHOULD YOU BE FRIENDS WITH?

Just as there are people you should avoid in order to enjoy a better life, there are people you should try to meet in order to improve your day. Tastes are different, of course, and how we choose the people we want to mix with depends on several factors. Nevertheless, in the long run there are certain types of people who are more pleasant to socialise with than others. It is life-enhancing to meet people who are *cheerful and positive*. Being together with people you can have fun with raises your spirits. After mixing with people like that, you feel like a dried-out pot plant that has just been watered. We also become more cheerful and positive after a session with these human labradors. (But note that "cheerful and positive" doesn't necessarily apply to a manically giggling wag who insists on telling you jokes about the vicar and the two candidates for confirmation.) It's more a matter of meeting people who radiate an aura of warmth and happiness, rather than semi-professional stand-up comedians.

Cheerful and positive people are at the opposite pole to the miserable gits we all come across now and again. Our positive friends come back from holiday and say: "That was terrific. Two superb weeks. To be sure, we had a bit of bad luck with the weather – sleet all the time, the likes of which they haven't had in the Canary Isles for 126 years. But it didn't matter. Instead of swimming and sun bathing we did lots of other fascinating things. The food wasn't all that good at the hotel – we had four bouts of food poisoning, but one evening they had a marvellous pudding that was just about edible. There was a hole in the roof and our ceiling was leaking, but we stuffed my swimming trunks into the gap and repaired it. I sprained my ankle the day we arrived – the hotel staircase was a death trap. But it didn't really matter, you can always manage to limp your way through life after all. It really was a terrific holiday."

A couple of your friends are really miserable old gits, and when you meet them, they tell you about their holiday. "Bloody awful! We spent two weeks on Mallorca – non-stop sunshine, far too hot. The hotel food was nothing like what we're used to at home, and a couple of times they didn't serve the wine at the right temperature. Nobody at the hotel could speak English, and the receptionist was wearing a really ugly uniform. The chamber maid didn't understand a word I said to her, despite the fact that I spoke very loudly and slowly. Geraldine bought a vase that didn't fit in at all when we got it home, and I burnt my back red raw in the sun. An absolutely awful holiday!"

Cheerful and POSITIVE people are at the opposite pole to the miserable gits we all come across now and again.

It's also uplifting to mix with people who are *outgoing and generous*. Not necessarily generous in the material sense, but spiritually generous, people who open themselves up to you. People who don't hide behind masks and attitudes, but are straightforward and forthcoming.

Fair dinkum types are sometimes considered to be a bit boring (and they sometimes are); but it makes sense to knock about with fair dinkum people. There's something reliable and secure about them, even if they aren't always overflowing with wit and joviality. There's a lot to be said for getting drunk with a fair dinkum type, then discussing life or woollen socks with him.

Just as it's a mistake to mix with nasty people, it's good to mix with *nice people*. To be sure, it's a back-handed compliment to say about somebody that: "He's a very nice man, no matter what." It sounds as if the person you are talking about is a hopeless berk with no saving graces – but "he's a nice man, no matter what". This is most unfair. Being nice is a grossly undervalued quality. It's not wimpish to be nice, being nice is estimable and admirable. Nice people don't say nasty things about you the moment you leave the room, and they don't try to make your life a misery. A nice person stands by you and comes to your aid when required. He lends you his umbrella even when it isn't raining.

✪

ONLY BELIEVE AMUSING RUMOURS

We are always bombarded with rumours. Rumours blossom forth in newspapers, on the television and in the coffee room at work. No rumour is too incredible to spread and take root.

"Have you heard that Cilla Black's pregnant?"

"Cilla Black? That's not possible! She must be over 60!"

"It's true! My friend's husband has a mate who lives next door to somebody whose pal knows for certain. She's four months gone."

"You don't say? Who's the father?"

There are good rumours and bad rumours, and both kinds spread like wildfire. Your life will be better if you make up your mind to believe only good rumours. Amusing rumours are true, "no smoke without fire", but it's not worth bothering about bad rumours – "they're just empty gossip, there's no truth in them, none at all". Notable among the positive rumours you ought to believe are all the exciting gossip about celebrities, about the woman next door and the postman, and the pay rise that everybody at work is going to get. No smoke without fire – of course that well-known actor has an alcohol problem and is too fond of little boys. There's no doubt the postman looks het-up when he says hello to Beatrice Johnson on the third floor, and there's definitely talk about a 15% pay rise. Good rumours, therefore true.

On the other hand there's no reason at all to believe vague rumours about redundancies at work, an imminent recession, or research that suggests it's dangerous to drink water. You can ignore such rumours altogether. The same applies to rumours suggesting that your partner has found somebody else, or that your partner knows that you've met somebody else. The rumour that teeth with the old type of amalgam fillings can explode is obviously wrong if you have such fillings, but true if you don't while your boss does. Similarly, rumours about a big hike in the interest rate are quite wrong if you have large loans, but true if you have money in the bank.

You should believe all rumours about the Queen and the Duke of Edinburgh, and all rumours about television stars and top politicians. Life is much more enjoyable if you know which passing rumours to believe, and which can be dismissed with a snort: "Huh, I wouldn't believe daft rumours like that for one second! I don't understand how people can believe such rubbish! Idiotic! Mind you, I did hear – and I have this on very good authority – that Princess Anne and Cliff Richard…"

❁

DON'T BE AFRAID OF MAKING A FOOL OF YOURSELF

We're all afraid of making a fool of ourselves in various circumstances. We don't want to lose face, become a laughing stock or feel that everybody is pointing at us. (Always assuming we're not a politician – if we are, then all that is routine.) We often refrain from doing something for fear of putting our foot in it. But if we are always afraid of making a mistake, we'd never get much done. And besides, how important is it in fact, always to try to make sure that were are successful and perfect?

So what, if we occasionally do something silly?

Everybody does. We can't stagger through life, constantly scared to death of making a fool of ourselves. "What if I say something stupid?" "What if I do something stupid?" "What if I blush, fall asleep, belch or lose my trousers? Or do all of those things at the same time?"

We should try to be generous with ourselves, and not be glancing furtively around all the time, thinking: I hope I haven't just done something stupid. If we open up a little bit and are a bit more straightforward with others, the people we are with will also unbutton a bit. Being open with others doesn't mean talking non-stop about yourself all the time, but rather just being yourself in an honest and straightforward manner.

But what if some people don't like us the way we are?

What if other people start laughing at you when you talk about what you like, think and feel? Well, there's always a risk that will happen; but if it does, you're not the one at fault. It's the other person who is demonstrating his small-mindedness by trying to criticise you or ridicule you. You can safely ignore people like that. Most people you meet won't act like that at all. They'll be pleased that you are being open with them, especially if you make it clear that you would appreciate it if they were open with you. A lot of people are like old-fashioned water pumps: you have to pour a little of your own water into them first before they can start producing water from their own well. (This is a figure of speech, and has nothing to do with the fact that some people unbutton themselves more easily if you pour some alcohol into them instead of water.)

❁

NOT EVERYBODY'S RIGHT, YOU KNOW

It could be as well to know that not everybody is always right. When people have different views about something, there is often a tendency among third parties to try to compromise, and to suggest that both of the antagonists are right.

"Charlie is absolutely right. But Pete, who has diametrically opposed views, is also absolutely right."

Oh yes? How can both of them be absolutely right? And why should they be?

Sometimes it can get a bit absurd. "Oh, so Eric says that seven times seven is forty-nine and Matt says it's fifty-six. No doubt the truth of the matter is somewhere in between, so the right answer should be fifty-three."

But in many circumstances the plain fact is that one of them is absolutely right, and the other is absolutely wrong.

(For those of you who never mastered your multiplication tables, seven times seven is forty-nine.)

> "Charlie is ABSOLUTELY right. But Pete, who has diametrically opposed views, is also ABSOLUTELY right."

❋

EXPECT NOTHING! (OR DO THE OPPOSITE)

Life is full of adversity.

If it's not one thing, it's the other. Sometimes it's both at the same time. On our journey from the cradle to the grave, a single ticket, we come up against all kinds of misfortunes. Some are major, some are minor, and others are simply daft.

We do whatever we can in order to overcome the obstacles, but we don't always succeed. The higher our expectations, the harder our fall if things don't turn out as we'd expected. We hope to become Wimbledon Champion, but the nearest we get to that is the quarter-finals of the junior championships for Chipping Sodbury and District. We hope to win the Nobel Prize for Literature, but the nearest we get to that is a shared third prize in the *West Wales Evening News* short story competition on the theme "My Pet". We go all out to become a new Elvis Presley or Michael Jackson, but we are booed off the stage at the Beck Hole Church Hall when we trip over the microphone cable while singing "Yesterday". The audience (all 37 of them) split their sides with laughter, and the following day we return with heavy hearts to our day job as a comprehensive school caretaker.

There is a good way of coping with adversity.

Expect nothing!

If you never expect anything, you're never disappointed. If you assume that everything will go wrong, you're not disappointed when it does. And if by any chance it doesn't, you are all the merrier. If you assume the positive stance of "this is bound to go wrong", you can take on any challenge you care to name.

If you take it for granted that you'll fail to qualify for the local caber-tossing championship, but get through to the final and finish sixth, you'll be overjoyed. The sixth prize is half a kilo of coffee, and you celebrate, even though you don't drink coffee. If you'd aimed at winning the competition, you'd have been bitterly disappointed by your sixth place, especially as there were only eight entrants. But by setting your sights low, you are pleasantly surprised instead.

There is another way of coping with adversity, but that's a bit more difficult. Do the opposite. Start off by assuming that everything will turn out for the best, no matter how unrealistic that might seem. Assume that everything you do will end up by being a fantastic success, that you'll win every competition you enter and that everybody you meet will be nice and friendly. If you take that approach you'll be constantly disappointed, and before long you'll be so chastened that nothing will get to you any more. However, this is not an especially good way of doing things. It's better to hope that you're going to be last, and then you'll be so happy when you come last but one.

❂

"WHAT IF A METEOR FALLS ON MY HEAD?"

There's no point in going around worrying about things that might never happen.

It's just a waste of energy. If you spend all day worrying if you're going to be hit by a meteor, you're wasting time that could usefully be spent doing something else. There's so much we worry about that's never going to happen. It's better to face up to problems when they actually occur, rather than wasting time and effort worrying about something that's never going to come to pass.

There are lots of things you can worry about unnecessarily.

"What if war breaks out? What should we do then? Shouldn't we find out the location of the nearest air raid shelter?"

"What if I'm made redundant? What would I do then? I'd have to try to find a new job. How would I go about that? Maybe it's best to start looking for a new job now. Just to be on the safe side."

"What if I get kicked on the head by an ostrich? I've read that ostriches pack a very nasty kick. Not that there are any ostriches where I live, but still. An ostrich might escape from a circus or a zoo. As I'm walking through town, an escaped ostrich might suddenly come hurtling towards me and kick me on the head. Maybe we should all wear helmets when we go to town?"

"What if I get ingrowing toenails? I might not be able to wear my new shoes. Eric's brother got ingrowing toenails, it was extremely painful. At least, I think it was ingrowing toenails he had. It might have been water on the knee. What if I get water on the knee?"

There's no limit to what you can start worrying about.

"What if the world comes to an end? I read in the paper

that there's a risk the sun might explode – then what would happen? It probably wouldn't be enough to cover yourself with sun cream, even if it was factor 32. But the opposite might happen – we might find ourselves in a new ice age. I happen to have a very thick woollen jumper from Iceland, but I don't suppose that would help much. Just think what would happen if the world came to an end – who would then take care of my allotment?"

If you insist on worrying about something, wait until there's something to worry about.

If you spend all day WORRYING if you're going to be hit by a meteor, you're WASTING time that could usefully be spent doing something else.

DON'T GO TO THE OPERA

Unless you are a fanatical opera fan, you should avoid going to the opera. For ordinary people who are not in love with operas, going to see one can be almost unbearable. It starts at seven o'clock. After three hours of the performance you check your watch: it's twenty minutes past seven. No, there's nothing wrong with your watch.

It doesn't matter which opera you go to see, they are all long and painful. The characters on the stage sing very loudly and for a very long time in a most unnatural way. Our voices are not made to sing opera, nor are our ears made to listen to it. Operas are often performed in a foreign language, which doesn't make them any more enjoyable. Even if the cast are singing in English, you can't hear a word they say. Shrill falsetto voices reduce your eardrums to narrow shreds, and long notes remind you inevitably of lovelorn tomcats in March. Time passes painfully slowly, and you wonder why on earth you allowed yourself to be persuaded to go to the opera. You are reminded of the fact that someone once said: "If you take your seat in the opera house before the performance has finished, you've arrived in time."

It's difficult to sleep while watching an opera. The sound level is usually very loud, and the performers really do belt it out. If you are forced to go to an opera, therefore, the trick is to find the right seat.

"Can you hear every note clearly here?"

"Oh no, these are good seats."

Nobody knows why opera singers can't sing like ordinary people, but in private a lot of opera singers are very pleasant and it's quite safe to entertain them in civilized surroundings.

❂

"TO BE OR NOT TO DO"

Early on in life we have to be good and do certain things. We have to empty our plates, clean our rooms, do our homework, take the rubbish out to the dustbin and stop beating up our younger brother. When we grow up we're also expected to do things all the time: get a job, get married, have children, take the rubbish out to the dustbin, get divorced and wash the car. A bit later on in life we're expected to get a better job, remarry, save towards our pensions and take the rubbish out to the dustbin. We're expected to do something all the time. And if we don't do anything, we're expected to do something else.

We have to learn to be, without doing anything!

We have to be able to take a break, not just from work, but also from the constant feeling we have to be doing something. Hamlet never said, "to be or not to do"; nor did he say "to be or not to be, what should I do now?". Hamlet no doubt had other things to think about, what with all his flawed family relationships and his Ophelia. But the rest of us ought to bear in mind that it's not just a matter of "to be or not to be", but also "to do or not to do". All the time

> We have to be able to take a BREAK, not just from work, but also from the constant feeling we have to be doing something.

we're worrying about doing something, which means that we sometimes forget just to be.

What do you do when you just want to be?

It may seem an unnecessary question, but it isn't for some people. There are some individuals, and there are quite a lot of them in fact, who don't know what to do in order just "to be". They're so brainwashed into always having to do something that they simply don't know how to shake off the more or less compulsory instruction always to be busy. Most often it's their work that they "have to" do, even in their leisure time; but whenever they are free, they feel they have to "do something". They have to work out, or go to French lessons, or repaper the bedroom. There's nothing wrong with these occupations: working out is good for you, it's useful to be able to order "un café au lait", and the bedroom really does need repapering. (The old paper with all those enormous snakes in orange and mauve gave you nightmares.) But you have to be able to shake off your work, without replacing it immediately with French or wallpaper.

Doing nothing.

Not even giving a thought to what you ought to be doing, or what you should do tomorrow. Just relaxing, and being. The answer to Hamlet's immortal question, "to be or not to be", is "to be". If you find it hard just to be, without doing anything, you can always take the rubbish out to the dustbin. But try to give that a miss as well.

❁

TRAVEL FIRST, WIN LATER

"When I win the National Lottery, I'm going on a round-the-world trip!"

"When I win the Football Pools, I'm off to the Maldives!"

"When I win the Women's Institute raffle, I'm going to Milton Keynes!"

Lots of people want to undertake that dream trip, and resolve to go there when they win some money. "When I've won, I shall…"

That's wrong.

If you put off travelling until you've won the pools, the Lottery, on the gee-gees or whatever form of gambling you prefer, you'll most probably never go anywhere.

Do it the other way round!

Travel first and then win later.

But what if you don't win later?

Well, you've had your trip – and that was the most important thing after all.

✸

EAT SOMETHING BAD FOR YOU!

Oh yes, we all know we should eat something that's good for us. (It even says that in this book, in the *"Healthy Health Nagging"* chapter.) But there is a limit to how much doing what's good for you and other self-flagellation you can stand. You can't spend the whole of your life eating sultana bran and bean sprouts. Just occasionally you need to indulge in something tasty that's bad for you. Besides, who says it's bad for you? If it tastes nice it's good for your soul, and your body's attached to your soul and so it must be good for your body as well. In a way.

The things you decide to eat that are bad for you but good for your soul naturally vary from person to person. Chocolate mousse, strawberry ice cream, cream buns or chips with bearnaise sauce are uplifting for any number of people. After a large dollop of chocolate mousse, life seems to be simpler to cope with, despite the depressing news the scales have to impart. A good set of scales would weigh both your body and your soul, but unfotunately the ones we have don't do that.

> After a dollop of CHOCOLATE
> mousse, life seems simpler,
> despite the depressing news the
> scales have to impart.

If you think it's wrong, and bordering on the sinful, to eat things that are bad for you, then you have a bad conscience when you've finished eating. That is how you atone for your sins. First you eat a large portion of beef, chips and bearnaise sauce, and you follow that with a dessert comprising whipped cream and chocolate sauce. Then you say to yourself: "That was stupid. I shouldn't have eaten all that. It was really stupid to sit there and devour all that. I really must stop forcing all these cholesterol bombs into me. It really isn't good for me. I'll have to put a stop to it. That's it. Never again. I'll just finish off the rest of the whipped cream. Wasn't there a bit of chocolate sauce left?"

✲

THE WORLD IS NOT BLACK AND WHITE

Is your life like a chessboard?

Rectangular, and black and white? Populated with beings that are either black or white?

If so you should change either your glasses or your way of looking at things.

The world is not black and white. People, ideas or actions are rarely completely black or white, but have every imaginable shade of grey and other colours dotted around. It's often convenient to divide the world into black and white – it becomes easier to understand if we do that. We decide that some people are good, and others are evil. Some countries are on the ball, others are rubbish. Whoever isn't for us is against us. We make up our minds what's black and what's white, and we stick to that. Charlie's a good bloke, even if he says daft things now and again. But Nick's an unpleasant type – he sometimes says daft things.

Life becomes easier if we accept that not everything is black or white.

(Life would be even easier if everything were in fact black or white, but unfortunately that's not the case.) Most things are wishy-washy colours, or striped, or chequered. Very few people are dyed-in-the-wool black or white. Most people we know are not too bad on the whole, although they can be a bit annoying or petty at times. Some people are rather annoying, but can be quite pleasant at times. Obviously there are some genuine saints, or the opposite; but most people are somewhere in between, a sort of black-and-white chequered colour.

Once we have made up our minds that somebody or something is totally white or totally black, we prefer not to see anything that suggests something different. That would only complicate matters. We don't want to know that our idol has a degree in paedophilia, or that the person we most like to hate donates money to poverty-stricken children. That just muddies the waters. Black should be black, and white should be white.

But that is rarely the case in fact.

This doesn't only apply to people. A non-profit-making charity turns out to spend nearly all the money it receives on wages for its employees – who would have thought it? And just to make things more complicated, people sometimes turn green.

What should we make of that, then?

What we need to do is to accept that most things are not either-or, but both-and. After all, grey is quite a nice colour. Not to mention dark white.

✱

TODAY IS A FINE DAY!

Carpe diem is not, as many people think, a fisherman's term meaning "catch the carp". *Carpe diem* means "seize the day", suggesting that you should make the most of every moment. Live in the present, not yesterday or tomorrow or the day before yesterday.

A lot of people say: "Next week I'll… Next year I'll… One fine day I'll…"

Today is a fine day!

You should make the most of every moment, live in the present. There's no point in grieving over yesterday or worrying about tomorrow. Yesterday's been and gone, and we don't know what will happen tomorrow. All you have is the here and now, and you must make the most of that now. Of course, it's sometimes easier said than done, especially if you happen to have toothache here and now. Then it's easier to hanker after yesterday when you didn't have toothache, or long for tomorrow when you'll have had your tooth filled, with any luck.

When it's cold and grey and dark, we long for the summer that's past or the summer that's coming, instead

Most people we know are not too bad on the whole, although they can be a bit ANNOYING or petty at times.

of "seizing the day". But today is the only thing we can be more or less sure about. We might not remember yesterday, and even if we do we can't change anything. And who knows what will happen tomorrow? It might rain. It's best to make the most of today.

There is a saying that "today is yesterday tomorrow". You could also say "yesterday was today tomorrow". Or "today was tomorrow yesterday". The day before yesterday was today the day after tomorrow and yesterday will be the day before yesterday tomorrow. But what good does it do to bandy days back and forth like that? It gets you nowhere, and you ought to have paid the electricity bill the day before yesterday. You'll have to do it tomorrow instead, but as tomorrow will be yesterday the day after tomorrow, you might as well wait until the reminder comes.

The important thing is that you make the most of today! Who knows what bills you'll receive tomorrow?

❂

HURRY UP AND CALM DOWN!

"Death is nature's way of telling you that you should calm down a bit."

Stress is not good for you. In recent years there has been more and more talk about stress and burn-out. There's no limit to the ideas and advice you can get on this subject. What you should do, what you shouldn't do – and how on earth can anybody manage to read everything that's been written about stress? It's very stressful to try to keep up with all the new discoveries and theories concerning stress, and all the research into burn-out and burning the midnight oil. If you were to concentrate all the advice and research results about stress into a single sentence, it would be: Calm down!

Calming down a bit means not getting unnecessarily worked up about things (such as new and alarming reports about stress), and learning that nothing is as urgent as you think. You can also learn that you don't have to keep on striving upwards the whole time. (Surely you don't want to get to heaven all that urgently – stress will only bring forward the arrival date.) You should work your way through what you have to do, put aside what's unnecessary, and then do what really needs to be done at your own pace.

The only thing you need to hurry up with is calming down.

✦

SWIM WITH DOLPHINS

It's a well-known fact that swimming with dolphins makes you feel good, physically and mentally. In recent years scientists have been able to prove that this is not merely a myth. By registering the tiny electric currents in the human brain (EEG-measurements), they demonstrated that dolphins do in fact affect the human brain. Being together with dolphins does us good. Dolphins are also intelligent animals – many people maintain that they are more intelligent than humans. And there are in fact reasons to suspect this might be true: who is it that queues up and pays good money to watch the other one playing?!

> By registering electric currents in the human brain, they demonstrated that dolphins do AFFECT the human brain.

Unfortunately it can be difficult to keep dolphins in your home, even if you do have an unusually large bathtub. (Keeping a tin of tuna is not an adequate substitute.) You have to try to arrange your swimming sessions with dolphins in some other way, such as in a dolphinarium where guest swimmers are allowed.

If you don't have access to dolphins, you can always stroke a cheerful labrador instead. That has almost the same uplifting effect. (It doesn't have to be a labrador, other breeds of dog can serve just as well.) But best of all is a labrador puppy bubbling over with joy. Stroking a puppy like that has an immediate uplifting effect, and very soon you will find yourself wagging your own spiritual tail in delight. Ideally, depressed people should spend at least ten minutes every day stroking a labrador. And all other people as well.

❁

THE WORLD IS FULL OF FOOLS

There are an awful lot of fools in the world, and you should try to keep away from them. That's not so easy as they are everywhere. You're bound to have at least one or two at your workplace. Your boss is often a real fool. How on earth could he have become your boss? Intrigue and croneyism, of course. He's shored up by other fools. There is every reason to believe that there exists a secret network of incompetent fools who help each other. You find these fools in all layers of society. Surprisingly many of them are politicians, and several of them are in the government. Just look at how the country's run! Fools, fools, fools, wherever you look you see fools.

Many fools have a predilection for working in the public sector. They especially like working for the Inland Revenue, the Department of Health and Social Services, or as traffic wardens. There are also fools with an interest in sport: they work as football referees, hockey umpires or line judges at tennis matches. These sporting types almost always suffer from impaired eyesight. It's beyond comprehension that they are allowed to keep their jobs, as they are almost blind and also mentally challenged. Intrigue and corruption, of course. You might also wonder why so many fools are allowed to have a driving licence. They can't drive a car, don't know the Highway Code, and always drive too fast or too slow. The authorities ought to do something about these car-driving idiots – but unfortunately, so many people working for the authorities are fools.

It's hard dealing with fools, especially as most of them don't realise they are fools: this makes all contact with them very difficult. A fool doesn't realise he is a fool.

How do you know yourself if you're a fool?

That's a difficult question to answer, but of course, you aren't one. All the others are, though.

GET YOURSELF A GOOD DOCTOR

Life is easier if you have access to a good doctor.

But what is a good doctor?

Is it a doctor who does what patients want him to do? A doctor who signs sick certificates? Who prescribes tranquillizers in economy packs? Who has the latest magazines in the waiting room? Whose hands don't shake when he's operating?

As long as you're healthy, all doctors are good – in other words, as long as you don't need to consult them. But as soon as you feel ill, you'd prefer to meet a doctor who isn't related to Dr. Frankenstein. If you have stomach ache, a pain in your foot or somewhere over your head, you need a good doctor. When you have earache, a pain in your knee or in your soul, you don't want to see a doctor who says: "Cure your illness, Mrs. Johnson? I can't even pronounce it!"

We want a *good* doctor. So, how do we define that?

What qualities do we most want our doctors to have? There's an old joke to the effect that: "A good doctor needs to have three things: a confidence-inspiring appearance – and if he has that, the other two aren't necessary." That's not quite true. It's no doubt good if our doctors inspire confidence, but there again, some politicians, second-hand car salesmen and confidence tricksters do that as well. We require a bit more of our doctors. What is it most important for our doctors to have? Knowledge, interest, empathy, a friendly manner? Of course, that depends on what type of person we are ourselves. For some patients the most important thing is that the doctor should know a lot, but for others it's that he should be friendly and understanding. Some research suggests that many patients think it's more important for a doctor to be nice than to be competent! That's not really all that hard to understand. A "nice" doctor is one who cares about you, shows an interest in you. If he doesn't have much knowledge, then he makes an effort to find out, because he's interested in his patients. A nice doctor inspires confidence, and the patient feels he's being looked after. Nevertheless, being "nice" is not enough if that doctor keeps making mistakes because he doesn't know enough and has awful judgement.

"Well, Mr Johnson, take one of these tablets tonight and another one if you wake up tomorrow morning."

It's best to look out for a doctor who's nice but also competent and accessible. You should avoid doctors who are not interested in you, who don't seem to care, are rude, or whose potted plants die. (That last criterion can be difficult to apply nowadays, when there are such

natural-looking plastic plants available.) We don't want to see a doctor who sits there going through other patients' notes, cleaning his fingernails or looking at his watch all the time we're telling him about our stomach pains. We want a doctor who concentrates on what we have to say, takes all our pains and symptoms seriously, even when we think we've got vertigo in the knee. We want a doctor who can calm us down, comfort us and support us as we limp through life.

We want a doctor who oils the wheels of our life cycle.

ACCEPTING THE UNACCEPTABLE

This is one of life's most difficult lessons.

You have to learn to accept things that you think are totally unacceptable.

There is so much in life that you can find difficult to approve of. Not just difficult relatives, high petrol prices or the fact that your woollen sweater shrinks in the wash, despite the fact that the shop assistant who sold it to you swore blind it wouldn't. You sometimes need to go to the dentist, which is not particularly pleasant: but you have to accept that life is not just a bed of roses, but also comprises root fillings and inflammation of the gums.

Perhaps the most unacceptable aspect of life that we have to accept is that it comes to an end. And there is no appeal against this grim fact. Another grim fact that a lot of people find hard to accept is high taxes. If you can find a skilful financial adviser you might be able to avoid paying taxes, but it's rather more difficult to find a loophole when it comes to death.

It can be hard to accept that there is no divine justice in this world. Why does evil sometimes flourish but a

There is so much in life that you can find DIFFICULT to approve of. And not just difficult relatives.

good person stumbles and breaks his leg? Why does that malevolent Charlie get ahead at the expense of Pete, who is so nice? There are no satisfactory answers to any of these questions – at least, not answers we want to hear.

Nor is it always so easy to accept that time passes, that things and people change, and that nothing lasts for ever. Perhaps there are bits of yesterday that we would like to retain, but we can't. The world is constantly changing, and there's not much we can do about it. Buildings are demolished, friends disappear, and we lose our hair and our enthusiasm. All we can do is to grit our fists and clench our teeth, natural or dentist-made.

The easier you find it to accept facts you cannot accept, the better. There's no point in fretting about things you can do nothing about. Tilting against windmills will get you nowhere, you'll simply get dirty and out of breath. It's better to shrug off the deplorable state of affairs, and drink a cup of coffee. (But do you really have to accept the fact that the coffee tastes of detergent?)

❂

DON'T HARBOUR GRUDGES

A good memory is an excellent thing to have. But it's not such an advantage when it comes to remembering all the little injustices you've had to suffer, real or imagined.

It's unwise and futile to harbour grudges. Always bringing up the past often damages relationships that would otherwise flourish, and it embitters your life. You should try to make your life better, not bitter.

Going through life fuming about Nick, who bullied you at primary school, is a waste of energy. There's no point in going on and on about how Nick used to trip you up, throw snowballs at your head and stole your football. The same applies to your relationship with your colleague Leonard, who took all the credit for something you had done when you used to work together – that's 11 years ago now: how much longer are you going to go on thinking about that? You simply have to learn to bury what are really only minor details from your past life, and move on. Perhaps you could even make allowances, at least in Nick's case. His home life was a mess, and he was teased at school because of his protruding ears.

You must learn to accept the truth that the past is gone and done with.

You can't spend 30 years plotting revenge, or feeling offended by what Linda said to you in the summer of 1987. Forget it and move on. Besides, perhaps you remember it wrongly. Memory can play all kinds of tricks on you. Perhaps it wasn't how you remember it at all. In fact, it wasn't Nick who threw those snowballs at you, but Charles. And he was really throwing them at Eunice, but he missed and hit you instead. Nick wasn't even there: he was hiding away in a corner, crying his eyes out because Benny and Jack had been teasing him about his protruding ears.

> You can't spend 30 years plotting REVENGE, or feeling offended by what Linda said to you in the summer of 1987.

Naturally, there are some injustices and acts of malevolence that are so major and hurtful that they can never be forgiven; but even if you can't forgive them, you can put them behind you. And when it's a matter of trivialities, there's nothing positive about allowing such memories to make life a misery for you. The only one to suffer is you. Be a bit magnanimous, and forget all about Nick, Leonard and Linda.

Mind you, it's a completely different kettle of fish when it comes to Ronnie, Chris and Georgina – obviously you need to put them in their place if you get half a chance…

❂

POINTLESS LEISURE TIME?

What should we do with our leisure time in order to get ourselves a better life?

What shouldn't we do with our leisure time in order to get ourselves a better life?

How should we handle our free time in order to get as much benefit from it as possible? (The assumption is, of course, that we do have some free time. If you have small children and hence a few non-stop eating, screaming, crawling, nappy-change-demanding, non-sleeping, graffiti-scrawling little monsters, you probably don't have any major problems with leisure time. The same applies if you are a stressed-out workaholic with dollar signs in your eyes instead of pupils.)

But if you do have leisure time, what should you do with it? Of course, that depends on your ambitions and interests. You might like to go jogging and spend all your free time running through the forest till you are beautifully blue in the face and feel as if your chest is about to explode. Or you might prefer to get your exercise by means of some gentle ball game or other which involves you in a subtle means of spraining your ankles or straining your knees. Many people like to go to the gym and pump iron, strain their necks, pull a muscle or dislocate their shoulders. Exercise is good for you, and hence a good way of spending your free time.

If you have small children you might want to spend what little free time you have sleeping, or perhaps slumping back in a semi-comatose state in an armchair, watching television or staring at the wall, while wondering how many more years it will be before your children go to sleep at night. If you don't have small children who take up all your free time, you might like to devote it to reading books, going to the cinema, eating walnuts or surfing the Internet.

It's also fun to go for long walks, go for short walks, or sit in cafés wondering what you've made of your life.

A lot of people have a hobby that takes up all their leisure time. It's good to have a hobby, and have something to do while worrying about everything under the sun. There's no end of hobbies you could devote yourself to. Collecting various things is popular. You can collect stamps (but preferably not in front of an open window), sea-shells, pens, tin soldiers or wives. Some people collect money, but that doesn't count as a real hobby. Those with the knack like to build plasticine models or three-storey houses. Depending on how much interest and talent you have, you could also devote yourself to porcelain painting, wrestling or poetry. If you are multi-talented, you can devote yourself to porcelain painting, wrestling and poetry at the same time, as long as you make sure you don't put a fragile miniature vase in an arm lock.

Lonely people might enjoy playing patience. But if you do, make sure you don't do like the man who was playing patience and caught himself cheating. He got so angry, he never spoke to himself again.

Is there anything you shouldn't do in your spare time? If you have a pain in your foot, you shouldn't enter the marathon. If you suffer from hay fever, you shouldn't work on your stamp collection in the pollen season. If you collect wives, you should finish with one wife before starting on the next. The most important thing you should *never* do in your free time is work. Leisure time is when you're supposed to give work a rest, no matter whether you play golf, paint porcelain, sleep or collect stamps. It's important you stay away from work when you're free. If you work in your spare time, it's appropriate to talk about pointless leisure time.

❂

GO TO BED!

Human beings are the only animals that go to bed when they are not tired, and get up when thy are.

It's important to get sufficient sleep.

We all know that getting too little sleep is not good for us. People react in different ways to a lack of sleep. Some people become slightly manic. They become overactive, run around like a headless chicken and try to do 11 things at once. They polish the floor, read French, build Lego models and make porridge, all at the same time. Others become irritable and grumpy, and end up hissing like a cat at anybody within range.

"Would you like a cup of coffee?"

"Go to hell!"

Some people become depressed after a few sleepless nights. People don't function as they should if they don't get enough sleep. Research has been done on the problem, including an investigation into junior doctors in the USA. These junior doctors were subjected to tests, both when they had had a good night's sleep and when they had been on call and worked throughout the night. One of the tasks the doctors were required to carry out was ECG tests on various patients. Those who had enjoyed a good night's sleep interpreted the results correctly, but the ones who had no sleep at all made catastrophic errors. Would you like to be operated on by a surgeon who hasn't slept for a few nights in a row, or fly in an aeroplane with a pilot who has spent the whole of the previous night awake?

Forcing people to keep awake has been used as a method of torture. Not having an opportunity to sleep eventually becomes intolerable, and people exposed to such torture have gone out of their minds. We have to sleep. It's not possible to fool your body into going without sleep. You might get away with it for a short time, but then both body and soul react. So you need to get plenty of sleep – preferably in the right context.

"I dreamt that I was sitting in the House of Commons fast asleep – and when I woke up, I was."

You need to sleep whenever you get the chance.

"Doctor, I haven't slept a wink for 14 days."

"Goodness me! How do you feel?"

"I feel fine. Luckily I get plenty of sleep during the night."

Sleeping Beauty slept for an awful long time – but then, she got her prince. She'd never have got him if she hadn't slept long enough and hence been grumpy and disagreeable because of a chronic shortage of sleep.

Sleeping really well is a marvellous thing – it's just a pity you can't be awake and make the most of it.

> "I dreamt that I was SITTING in the House of Commons fast asleep – and when I woke up, I was."

❂

WHO SHOULD YOU AVOID?

On our journey through life we come across all kinds of
people. We meet happy ones, sad ones, tall ones, short ones,
handsome ones, ugly ones, and people with moustaches. It's
inevitable that we also meet types of people we ought to
avoid. There are certain people we should avoid meeting,
avoid mixing with and avoid coming anywhere near.

There are people who can make your life a misery
simply by being who they are. If you want a better life
(and who doesn't?), you should shun them like the plague.
The first type of person you should look out for is *nasty
people*. It doesn't matter why nasty people are nasty, the
important thing is that they *are* nasty. Their nastiness
offends and poisons other people. They sometimes try
to hide their spiteful comments behind a bad joke, so
that they can defend themselves if the person addressed
or anybody else complains about their behaviour. "I was
only joking," they say with an innocent smile, but the
malevolence gleams like knife blades in their eyes. They
were not joking at all, they were simply wrapping their
poisoned arrows in the thin silky cover of a joke. These
nasty people often think carefully before they speak, so
that they can say something even more spiteful than if
they had spoken without thinking.

Nasty people weep over your wounds in order to drip
salt into them. When you meet a nasty person you should
walk away, both literally and metaphorically. You should
not mix with spiteful people, it always leads to grief and
misery. A nasty person can stab you in the back and then
report you to the police for illegal possession of a knife.

A really nasty person was once bitten by a big
rattlesnake. It was awful to see how the snake then curled
up and died. The person it had bitten grinned in

> It doesn't matter why NASTY people are nasty, the important thing is that they ARE nasty.

satisfaction, and continued on his way. Is that the kind of person you want to invite round for dinner? It would no doubt be better to invite the rattlesnake. At least it would rattle before biting you.

Nasty people ought to take out fire insurance rather than life insurance – there's no doubt where they'll end up when they die.

Another type you should avoid is *stingy people.* Their stinginess doesn't only manifest itself in material stinginess, i.e. being mean with money, but also in spiritual stinginess. A seriously stingy person finds it hard to pay compliments or give encouragement to others. Mean people are generally both materially and spiritually stingy. A really stingy skinflint is stingy no matter how rich he happens to be. His unwillingness to part with money has nothing to do with the state of his finances.

It's not pleasant, dealing with skinflints. People who change their name to Ritz Hotel so that they have the same name as on their towels at home. Tight-fisted people who went on their honeymoon alone in order to save money. When you have done something good, they don't want to give you any praise. You might think that kind words don't cost anything, but if you are mean, you are really mean. They don't want to give you anything at all. They only thing they might consider giving you is their cold.

Another type to steer well clear of is *people who only talk about illness, death and misery*. There are people who love talking about things like that. They might appear to be perfectly pleasant and normal, but the moment they open their mouths, off they go.

"Did you hear about George? He dropped down dead on the spot last week. He was in very good health, but then he just fell over and died. He wasn't all that old – the same age as you in fact. And then there was Sammy, I heard he's had a massive heart attack. He must be a few years younger than you."

It's very depressing to hear about all those illnesses and deaths. Give a wide berth to these prophets of doom.

Jealous and envious people are also best avoided. It's only human to be jealous, but some people can be very human indeed. A famous actor once said: "If people's jealousy is a measure of success, then I've been fantastically successful."

Jealous people radiate bad feeling wherever they go. They grow annoyed and bitter if you seem to be contented and happy (which is a good enough reason always to give the impression of being contented and happy whenever you bump into them).

You don't need to be better off than your jealous friends for them to be jealous of you. Your envious friends can be richer than you, have a posher car, a shinier toaster and a vacuum cleaner with greater suction power than yours, but they still begrudge you your things even so.

Jealousy is often misdirected, which can be something to bear in mind if you yourself should fall victim to this human frailty. We only see what's on the surface, and become jealous of that. Look how rich he is, and what a posh car she's got, they seem to be very well off. But what is the reality like behind the façade? He has enormous debts, there's a major fault in the gearbox of her car, and when they are not at each other's throats, they are discussing the possibility of divorce. Is that something to be envious of?

Insincere people are very unpleasant to deal with. They give you a friendly smile and drench you in large dollops of honey-sweet flattery. Their artificial goodwill knows no bounds, and they swear their eternal friendship and loyalty in mealy-mouthed tones. The moment you leave the room they inform anybody who wants to listen that you are a worthless and unpleasant person, and they've heard from reliable sources that you're a drunkard, a drug addict, a regular customer of child prostitutes, and that you beat your wife. And you also have a terrible dress sense. But when you suddenly re-enter the room, your insincere friend says: "Oh, good to see you've come back. We were just talking about you. I was explaining how you are one of the finest people I've met in the whole of my life. I mean that most sincerely. That's a very smart suit you're wearing, by the way. You look good."

Being together with insincere people is about as pleasant as having a scorpion inside your shirt.

❁

DROWN YOUR MOTHER-IN-LAW!

No, no, not literally, of course. What kind of an impression would that give? Polluting lakes and rivers like that? And mother-in-law is so… er… nice. But in both films and books mother-in-law has generally been portrayed as a pain. (And then there are all those mother-in-law jokes:

"Nev, my mum thinks you are a bit effeminate."

"Huh, compared with her, I am.")

The mother-in-law symbolizes difficulties and problems in this connection, and the heading "Drown your mother-in-law!" means that you should try to drown your sorrows. Somebody (Mark Twain?) expressed it very well when he once said: "A lot of people give their sorrows swimming lessons instead of drowning them."

You must learn not to give your sorrows swimming lessons. Not to fertilize and encourage the problems, but as far as possible, to drown them. But not with booze. That's not a good idea. The problems you look at through the bottom of a glass are magnified. (Hence the concept of the magnifying glass.) Try to shrug off everyday worries, they are hardly ever so great and so difficult as they seem. You should also be aware that if you have several worries, it's generally the case that when one or two of them disappear, the ones remaining shrink. Worries are like cream cakes: you can cope with a few of them if they are not too big, but if there are too many of them, you start to feel sick.

We can't count on going through life without having to face up to problems and worries, but when those worries are thrashing around desperately in the water, we should throw them a concrete life jacket.

❂

BOOKS

Can you achieve a better life by reading books?

Yes, that's very possible. You can enter the land of dreams via the enchanted world of books. (That's not true of accountancy textbooks, though.) When you read a book you can enter a different world and be somebody else, or somebody else's, or somewhere else.

When you read a book you can experience excitement, happiness or emotional turmoil. You can learn new things, or just for a while forget whatever it is you want to forget. You can read the memoirs of famous people, which are often interesting, entertaining, and a pack of lies. There are books about everything. If you are interested in Albanian poets (how on earth did you become interested in them?), you can read books by them. If you are fascinated by Chinese 17th-century porcelain, there are plenty of books

about that. And if you want to read about how to get yourself a better life, there's bound to be a book about that.

As far as books are concerned, they cater for an almost infinite number of requirements and tastes. Some people like historical novels, others prefer books about how to repair pocket watches. (There are also people whose main interest is historical novels about people who repair pocket watches.) There is a book for everybody. Highly strung people might want to read books about how to tie knots, while others might prefer do-it-yourself books of the type "How to make over a pensioner" or "How to make fireproof aluminium underpants".

Aren't there a lot of bad books?

Certainly, there's no end of bad books – the only problem is that tastes differ, so who is going to decide which books are bad? The book you think is rubbish might be regarded by your neighbour as the best he's ever read. And vice versa. It's the same with books as it is with people. You can't understand why your neighbour could possibly have married that old trout, but he loves her. Or vice versa.

The only thing you can go by is what you think yourself. It doesn't matter if your favourite books are about upper class young women, sex murderers, chickens or steam engines, the important thing is that you read something that brings a bit of extra enjoyment into *your* life. Books can give you feelings of consolation, happiness and security. (If you are an author they can also give you headaches, spots and grey hair.)

✪

ACCEPT THAT YOU ARE THE WAY YOU ARE

There are people who have no problems at all when it comes to accepting that they are the way they are. These people are completely satisfied with themselves, and think they are – if not perfect, then as near as makes no difference. They go through life with the feeling that they are faultless, which is no doubt nice for them. But perhaps not always for those around them.

However, most of us think that we are not as perfect and faultless as we would like. It's not always easy to accept that you are the way you are. We look around and imagine that everybody else seems to be satisfied with themselves, while we have trouble in accepting how we are. Why aren't we more charming, better looking, taller, thinner, more intelligent, shorter, more sociable, stronger or less talkative? Why are we not more cheerful, less short-sighted, more serious and less shy? Not only that, but our ears are too big and our bank accounts too small.

The more comfortable we are with ourselves, the easier it is to feel comfortable with others. If we can accept that we are the way we are, we can have a better life. We must try to be satisfied with ourselves, even if we are the type that spreads butter on ginger biscuits and then dops them in coffee. (Eek!) We must accept the way we are, even if we're not sure how to spell tarpaulin. (Tarpauline? Tarpalling? Tarporlin?)

In order to accept the way we are, we must first know what we are like.

Do we know that?

Yes, on the whole; but not entirely. We see ourselves differently from the way those around us see us, and besides, we are different in different contexts. But that doesn't matter, it's our own picture of ourselves that matters in this context. In our own picture of ourselves, however, we must also include our faults and shortcomings. We don't need to exaggerate these faults and shortcomings (which many people do), it's sufficient to acknowledge that we have them. And having done that, we must accept that we have them and be happy to live with them.

But shouldn't we try to correct the faults we have?

Of course – and good luck to you! And when you've eventually established that it's not so easy to correct those shortcomings, you should do as has just been suggested and be happy to live with them.

People are often quite grown-up and mature before they see and acknowledge their less good sides. Some people never become sufficiently grown-up and mature, even if they live to be 107. The rest of us, who eventually (or very quickly) realise that we are not perfect, have to accept the fact. We are not the greatest, the best, the most handsome; but that doesn't matter. Hardly anybody is. And the ones who think they are, are not either.

Life is not dependent on being the best. If you don't accept that, you are only causing difficulties for yourself.

You are good enough as you are!

But even so you could try to change some of your worst bad habits. Do you really need to belch loudly in public?

✪

WHAT ABOUT YOUR FAMILY?

As we all know, it's important to choose the right parents. That's not as easy as it sounds. When you're old enough to realise that you've chosen a couple of parents of questionable quality (probably acquired at sale prices), it's a bit late to do anything about it. Unfortunately you can't take your parents back and get a new pair. You have to make the most of what you've got. The same applies to your brothers and sisters. But what about your relations in general? Do you really have to mix with them? Wouldn't life be a bit easier if you could forget about your cousin Edward? And then there's Uncle Gerald. There's an old saying that suggests "blood is thicker than water". That is a questionable assertion. It would be much better and closer to the truth to say that: "A good friend is better than a bad relative". OK, we made that one up. Let's make it stick by repeating it emphatically: *A good friend is better than a bad relative.*

You can't choose your relatives (yet another of nature's inbuilt shortcomings), but you can choose whether or not you want to associate with them. We are all descended from apes, but some relatives seem to be closer to their ancestors than others. We look at our family trees, and realise some relatives spend most of their time up trees.

It's best to avoid them.

❂

BE A BIT CHILDISH

It's a good thing if you can remain a bit of a child at heart and keep a few childish attitudes even when you are grown up. If we can retain a child's curiosity, enthusiasm and spontaneity even when we are old (old in this context means over the age of 28), life becomes rather more fun. We don't need to run around in short trousers or believe in Father Christmas simply because we remain a child at heart. (Mind you, there is no real reason why we should stop believing in Father Christmas and start believing in the taxman instead, just because we have grown up.)

We mustn't start worrying about what is called our "real age". Our real age is as old as we feel. (Which of course means that some mornings we are 102, but the rest of the time we are considerably younger.)

Being childish is being vital and curious about life. Daring to ask "why?" and "how?" without being ashamed is something positive. Daring to play, both metaphorically and literally, is rejuvenating. Being a bit childish is good for us, even if we don't necessarily have to go to such extremes as eating porridge with our fingers or drawing steam engines on the wallpaper.

There are some people who are born at the age of 40. Little uncles and aunts who become more uncle-like or aunt-like the older they become. Their adult lives are not cheered up by spontaneity, or curiosity, or mental short trousers. They never do anything mad or unexpected, and even when they are young children they point out that Father Christmas is really Daddy. Later in life they tell their own children that there's no such thing as Father Christmas, but even so they will get an educational building set and a model of the town library as a Christmas present. We probably live better lives, and longer ones, if we are a bit childish from birth to death.

IS THE GOAL IN THE WAY?

Some famous and very dead Chinese philosopher once said: "It is the way that is the goal." What the Chinese philosopher means is that it isn't the goal itself that is the goal, but the way to the goal that is the goal. That suggests that the goal is in the way. In the way of what? The clever philosopher doesn't tell us that, just that the way is the goal. Our efforts to reach the goal, the journey to the goal, is said to be the actual goal. But is that really the case? If we are going to Manchester to attend my cousin's wedding, is the train to Manchester really the goal?

Why? There isn't even a decent restaurant car on the train. What does the dead Chinese philosopher actually mean? That the goal and significance of our lives is to take the train to Manchester and eat plastic sandwiches washed down with tannic acid-enriched coffee? And what would my cousin in Manchester, the bride-to-be, have to say if we regard the train journey as the highlight of her wedding?

Why should the journey be the goal? Shouldn't we look again at all those ancient philosophers' confused thoughts? When is the journey the goal? If we take a package holiday to the Canary Isles, the journey isn't the goal. The goal is the Canary Isles, not sitting like sardines in a tin on a cramped aeroplane, having first had to wait for four hours at the airport because of a "technical fault". The journey isn't the goal. The goal is the goal. Don't believe all the aphorisms and words of wisdom that people spread around.

✿

DON'T BE IMPRESSED WHEN YOU DON'T NEED TO BE

What are you impressed by? Titles? Money? Big muscles? People who can whistle through their noses?

It's easy to be impressed by peoples' various skills, qualities or possessions – sometimes a bit too easy. It's silly to be impressed if you don't have to be. If you're impressed too easily and too often by other people, you risk feeling inferior – "Oh, they're all so clever!" – or jealous: "Why can't I be like that?".

There's no reason why you should react in that way.

Most of the time we're impressed, we don't need to be. For instance, what do impressive titles really mean? "Professor" sounds pretty grand. We envisage somebody incredibly clever, erudite and knowledgeable. There are some professors like that. There are also professors who are devious, narrow-minded, megalomaniacal, and who've become professors by stealing other people's research results, vilifying colleagues and sticking at nothing. There's no reason to be impressed by professors like that.

"Managing director" is a title that impresses a lot of people. What is a managing director? It could be anything from a clever and efficient organizer to a power-crazed psychopath with a crying need to assert himself. There's no need to be impressed by that title. "Consultant" is another attractive title that doesn't mean a thing. "Admiral" is a very fancy title that means you have lots of gold bands on your uniform and know how to steer a boat. It's rather doubtful if one ought to be impressed by that.

There are plenty of other things you would be foolish to be impressed by. It's no doubt nice to have a lot of money, but that's nothing to be impressed by. Should we be impressed by very wealthy people, irrespective of how they acquired their fortune? Should we really be impressed by a mafia godfather's millions, or a drug dealer's luxurious custom-built Ferrari?

Of course not.

What about fame? Is fame something to be impressed by? That depends on why somebody is famous. There's a difference between Mother Teresa and a soap opera star.

Nor should we be unnecessarily impressed by people who come out with lots of hard words in an attempt to appear intellectual giants. (See also the chapter *Watch out for naked emperors*.) Knowledgeable and clever people seldom need to advertise their erudition and wisdom by boasting in a way few can understand. It's the pretentious upstarts who need hard words and mangled sentences in order to present themselves as something they aren't.

Some people think that "we are what we have", i.e. if they have pots of money, a big house and an expensive car, that's something we should be impressed by. But that's not true, of course. You're not what you have, you are what you are. A rogue is a rogue and a good person is a good person irrespective of who has the shiniest shoes.

But should one never be impressed by other people?

Certainly one should, but not primarily by titles, material excess or doubtful fame. There's every reason to admire and be impressed by those who do good deeds on behalf of others, who make sacrifices and volunteer selflessly when they're needed. People who do what they have to do, and a bit more besides, without going round telling the rest of the world about it.

People like that are impressive.

Even if they don't have shiny shoes or a red Ferrari.

❂

YOUR JOB

What kind of job you should seek, or not seek as the case may be, is discussed in the chapters *Jobs to go for* and *Jobs to avoid*. As a general rule. you should try and find a job you enjoy doing. It's not much fun going to work every day for 30 years if you dislike what you do. Not even for 30 years.

Apart from work that gives you pleasure (at least at times), most of us also have to find a job that makes us a living. It's no good enjoying your work if your wages are too low.

"Good morning sir, I've come to ask for a rise."

"Really? What's your reason this time?"

"My children have somehow discovered that other children eat every day."

Different jobs vary in how demanding they are, and people don't work equally hard in all work places. There is a classical story of how a country cousin came to London and was shown round the capital by a good friend who lived there and worked for a big company. When they passed the gigantic building where his friend worked, the country cousin said:

It's no good COMPLAINING to your boss that the coffee in the automatic machine is so strong that it's almost IMPOSSIBLE to doze off in the afternoon.

"My word, what an enormous place! How many people work in there?"

"About 25% of them," said his friend wearily.

If you want to be promoted, you often have to put in a little more effort. It's no good complaining to your boss that the coffee in the automatic machine is so strong that it's almost impossible to doze off over your desk in the afternoon. If you have no idea about what kind of work you would like to do or are best suited for, you could take an aptitude test in order to find out. If the results indicate that you are most suited to a gap year, it would be as well to take it again. If you start a new job and discover you are two months behind in your work after being there for three weeks, you should consider going in for something else. The aim has to be to try to find a job that you can both cope with and enjoy.

The most important thing, irrespective of your job, is not to work yourself to death. The most profound aim and significance of life is not to work yourself to death. It can be as well to be aware of that. Mind you, the fear of overworking should not be taken to extremes. "I had a job as a mattress-tester for a big bed-making company, but I was forced to resign. I just couldn't cope with them waking me up for every tea break."

❂

SMILE! (BUT NOT ALL THE TIME)

Does life really get better if you smile?

Yes, probably. You see, when you smile two things happen. One is that you fool your body into thinking that you are happy, and that makes you happier. It is really true. You can fool your body with this kind of ploy. The face muscles that are smiling send smile signals to the brain and the brain, that knows no better, assumes that the smile is a sign of happiness. As your body and your soul (wherever that is located) are closely linked, the smile cheers up the soul – even if it's an "artificial" smile. That raises the question: am I smiling because I'm happy, or am I happy because I'm smiling?

The other thing that happens when you smile is that people around you become more pleasant. Somebody once said: "The shortest distance between two people is a smile." It's difficult to say if this is true, it no doubt depends on how you measure; but it's quite clear that if you smile and look happy, you get a better reception from people you meet. But should you go around all day with an idiot smile on your face? No, of course not. If you do, you run the risk of being locked up, or at the very least you'll be accused of being drunk. But nevertheless, there are lots of occasions when you can choose between smiling or not smiling, and then you might just as well smile. You feel a bit happier as a result, those around you become more friendly, and so you become even happier because others are friendly.

But there are occasions when you shouldn't smile. Occasions when you should look serious. For example, if you are at work and speaking to the boss without having a clue what you are talking about, you should look deeply serious. People find it easier to believe somebody who looks serious. In some strange way or other, people think

subconsciously: "He looks so gloomy and serious, he must know what he's talking about." If you look serious, that inspires confidence and implies you are reliable. And so you should avoid smiling when you are making a presentation of something you know nothing about. Frowning slightly is also a good idea.

"Well, I've checked that these new figures show an increase in the decrease, and the curve is on the decline albeit upwards during the second quartile, which comes just after the first quartile, percentage-wise."

"I see, aha. Well, then. You look as if you know what you're talking about."

When you leave the room, you can allow yourself a broad grin.

It's quite CLEAR that if you smile and look happy, you get a better reception from people you meet. But should you go around all day with an IDIOT smile on your face?

❋

HOW BIG ARE YOUR SHOES?

There's an old saying that goes: "Anybody with sore feet has no other problems."

There's a lot of truth in that. The same thought is illustrated by the following story.

A poor man is walking down the street, limping and pulling faces. It's obvious that every step is agony for him. A woman passing by notices him and feels sorry for him. She looks at the man's feet. It's obvious that the shoes he's wearing are far too small. She goes up to him and says: "Are you all right? You seem to have problems."

"Problems?!" says the man. "I'll tell you the mess I'm in. My wife has left me – she ran off with the postman. My son has dropped out of school and become a drug addict. My daughter is earning extra pocket money as a prostitute at the Grand Hotel, and I'm being chased up by the Inland Revenue for unpaid taxes."

"Oh dear!" said the woman, sympathizing. "That's awful. In addition to all that, I see you appear to be wearing shoes that are too small for you."

"Yes, these shoes are size 8 and I actually take 9 ½."

"But isn't it incredibly painful, wearing shoes as small as that?"

"Yes, it certainly is. I can hardly think about anything else when I'm wearing these shoes. The only pleasure I have left in life is coming home from work in the evening and taking off these blasted shoes. It feels so good."

Sometimes minor worries seem more urgent than major worries. It could make sense to be clear about which worries and problems are most significant, and in which order you should try to deal with them. There's no point in closing your eyes to the major problems and only trying to deal with the minor ones. It would be better to acquire the right size of shoe.

DO SOMETHING UNEXPECTED!

Doing something unexpected can enrich your life.

You break out of the everyday routine and do something that surprises both you and everybody you know. It feels like an innovation, something untested and different. Whatever you do that's so unexpected doesn't really matter, as long as it's different from the daily routine. For instance, you can take three sugar lumps in your coffee instead of two, which is what you normally take. Or you can climb Mount Everest. In both cases you are doing something unexpected.

There's so much you can do to surprise yourself. If you always go to work at the same time every morning, you can break the mould and go to work after lunch instead. Or not turn up at all. (Your boss is bound to appreciate such minor deviations from normal procedures.) Or you might prefer to change jobs and launch yourself as a fishmonger. Or it might be sufficient to change your hairstyle, or dye your hair an attractive shade of blue. The main thing is that you should do something unexpected.

If you're in the habit of getting drunk every Saturday night, you could shock both your body and your friends by

> Dye your hair, get DRUNK, wear brown shoes with a dark suit, and then CLIMB Mount Everest.

staying sober. On the other hand, if you are a tee-totaller, you could get blind drunk and shout and yell for all you're worth in the town centre. Everybody will be very surprised, no matter what.

Perhaps you've lived in the same place all your life. In that case, you could emigrate to Australia – that really would be doing something unexpected, especially if you haven't a clue what you'll be doing there. If you're reluctant to do something as drastic as that, you could simply wear a pair of brown shoes with a dark suit. If you feel an unusually strong urge to do something other than what is expected of you, you could combine several things. Dye your hair, get drunk, wear brown shoes with a dark suit, and then climb Mount Everest. The most important thing is that you enjoy yourself.

❂

ACCEPT THAT OTHER PEOPLE ARE WHAT THEY ARE

If it can sometimes be difficult to accept that you are the way you are, it is no less difficult to acknowledge that other people are the way they are. It's sometimes extremely difficult, more or less impossible. Gerald for instance is absolutely hopeless! How could we possibly accept that he's the way he is?! He's so evil that he could steal a dead fly from a blind spider. Not to mention Brenda! She's so unpleasant that not even her shadow wants to go anywhere near her.

It is sometimes difficult to accept that certain people are what they are, and that they think the way they do. But we ought to be a bit tolerant and generous and accept people's oddities and peculiarities. After all, we don't need to mix with evil Gerald or unpleasant Brenda. But on the other hand we can try to accept that Brian and Carol don't think the way we do, no matter what subject we're talking about, and that George is a bit odd and sly. Not everybody is the way we would like them to be, but we just have to make the best of it. We are all different, think differently and react differently. There's no reason to get worked up about people, whether we know them or not, simply because they are a bit different or don't fit into the mould we've fitted ourselves into.

Our basic rule should be that we accept that other people are what they are – but there are limits, of course. It's good to be tolerant and understanding, but we don't need to put up with anything at all. The evil-minded bullies, the narrow-minded bigots, the violent trouble-makers – there's no reason why we should accept their behaviour. It can be hard enough to accept our peculiar cousins, eccentric colleagues or barmy neighbours.

> How could we possibly ACCEPT that he's the way he is?! He's so evil that he could STEAL a dead fly from a blind spider.

Not to mention our spouse. Do we really have to put up with the way he or she behaves? Actually yes, we do. Or at least, try our best to do so.

It's silly and impractical to always try to find fault with other people.

"I don't like that Evelyn at all!"

"Really? Why not?"

"I don't know yet, but I'll think of something."

DRESS HOWEVER YOU LIKE

A lot of people feel the need to follow changing fashions. This applies to both men and women (even if women are more addicted in this context). One year your skirt should be long and your tie wide, but the next year the fashion designers proclaim that your skirt should be wide and your tie narrow. We are informed that the autumn colours are "peacock blue" and "Indian green". What is "Indian green"?

We naively squeeze our feet into small torture chambers of leather, since fashion prescribes pointed toes. We get corns and hammer toe, but we are in fashion. We spend a fortune on a new suit with a three-buttoned jacket, despite the fact that our suit from last year looks good and is still in good condition – but last year's jacket had only two buttons. Why do we have to have three buttons, what's wrong with a two-buttoned jacket?! It's unfashionable: whatever will people say if we turn up in a suit like that?! But it's smart, it fits perfectly and it's very high quality. So what? It only has two buttons.

Two buttons!

Some higher power (God? The Government? UN?) has decided that suit jackets must have three buttons this year. We can't possibly risk our good name and reputation by appearing in public wearing a two-buttoned jacket. We don't want to be made fun of, made a laughing stock and scoffed at as we stand there in our pitiful two-buttoned suit, squirming in shame. Better to be dead than disgraced. And so we buy a new suit.

We go in for tight-fitting clothes that are sweaty and uncomfortable if that's what fashion dictates. We go in for clothes that are far too big – garments in which we can take two steps forward before the clothes start moving – if that's what the fashion designers have decided. We buy clothes that make us look like blithering idiots, or clothes that do more than just suggest we are completely colour blind, because they are fashionable. We would prefer to walk naked through town than wear a jacket with lapels that are too wide. And as if that weren't enough, we pay through the nose for these clothes. We are prepared to sell our soul to the devil in order to acquire the right label on our gear. (See also the chapter entitled *"Watch out for naked emperors"*.) With our finances in ruins, wearing narrow shoes that hurt our feet and a black coat of stonewashed sackcloth that's beginning to fall apart, we go to town and meet our friends. Our friends smile grimly in an attempt to conceal the fact that they are broke, their feet hurt, and they are freezing cold in the bitter wind that is blowing straight through their stonewashed sackcloth coats.

Life is much easier if we wear the clothes we feel comfortable in, even if they have two buttons instead of three. If one of our friends were to point in horror at our jacket and say: "For God's sake! Have you only two buttons?!", we would be able to say calmly: "Haven't you heard? It's all change. Two buttons are in again."

Then we could give our friend a tranquilizer and help him or her home.

❋

LISTEN TO OTHERS

Winston Churchill once said: "One of the most important lessons that life has taught me is that idiots are often right."

He had a point.

Sometimes people you expect to talk rubbish say something sensible. And you are surprised. That's why it's not a good idea to have preconceived ideas about what other people are going to say. It makes sense to listen to what others say, and not to listen only to yourself. Even a blind hen can find a grain of corn with the aid of a stick.

Both crazy Chris and boring Bert can say something interesting or touching, but we have to listen to them in order to understand what it is. We can't just block our ears because Chris only ever talks rubbish and Bert is so boring that he even makes clocks stop.

It also makes sense to remember that if we are talking to somebody who goes on about something he or she thinks is important or interesting, we should pay attention even if we think that what is being said is hardly riveting. We should resist the temptation to interrupt the other person in order to start talking about something *we* think is worth talking about. If the people we are talking to think that what they're talking about is relevant, we should be decent enough to listen to them. There might actually be something in what they say that we approve of. Besides, if we listen to what the other people say without interrupting them, perhaps they'll listen to us when we start talking about our own pet subject, 18th-century French porcelain.

It's never wrong to listen to what others have to say. It's also a fact that good listeners are well-liked because they listen. Harpo Marx writes in his memoirs about how he was accepted in a society of very talented intellectuals in which he felt at first very much like an outsider, only having attended school for two years. Harpo tells us that he was a good listener, and hence was not only accepted by the intellectual giants who never stopped talking, but also became very popular. (Harpo was not only a good listener, but also an enthusiastic croquet player, poker player and billiards player – which also went down well.)

With Harpo Marx in mind, one might well ask who would be most popular on social occasions: a person who listens to what others have to say, or one who keeps on interrupting to inform everybody that "I went through something much worse than that!". Most people prefer to talk about themselves and what they think and do, than about somebody else's life and experiences. All you need to do is to make yourself comfortable, lean back and listen – and you'll become popular.

We can't just BLOCK our ears because Chris only ever talks rubbish and Bert is so boring that he even makes clocks stop.

✿

BREAKING UP OR BREAKING DOWN?

If you are unlucky you can land up in a situation in which your existence feels like a boa constrictor squeezing the life-blood out of you. It feels as if you are slowly being choked, and no matter how much you wriggle and squirm, you can't get away. If the boa constrictor eases off a little, that's only because it's summoning up more strength for a new attack. Life feels like a grievous, stressful affliction, and your soul is gasping desperately for air. It's difficult to see clearly and there's a ringing in your ear – but nobody replies so it keeps on ringing.

> Surely you don't want
> to spend the rest of your
> life WRESTLING with a
> giant snake?

Not infrequently this boa-constrictor feeling is a result of being in a life situation that is becoming increasingly intolerable. It can be due to a wretched relationship with your partner, a stressful situation at work or some other problem connected with those close to you spiralling out of control. But most often it is your relationship with your partner or a seemingly hopeless situation at work that's behind it all. As if the boa constrictor squeezing you more and more tightly were not enough, you are also stranded in a swamp of quicksand into which you are sinking with gathering speed.

What to do?

If you have tried every conceivable way out, including crying for help, and nothing gets better even so, you have just two alternatives.

You can break up or break down.

It seems to make more sense to break up, even if that can be very painful. But if you are gradually being smothered by your relationship or your work, you don't really have much choice. If you have tried every other possible solution without success, it's better to break up than to break down. Surely you don't want to spend the rest of your life wrestling with a giant snake?

A life without boa constrictors in the quicksand awaits you just round the corner, even if the way there can be difficult at first. You shouldn't be scared of starting a new life, especially if your present one is too stressful and painful. It's a matter of gritting your teeth and starting out. Think of the old saying: "Stand on your own two feet, otherwise somebody else will."

❂

DON'T GET ANGRY OVER TRIFLES!

The world is full of annoyances. Nobody knows what function they have, apart from trying our patience. It's difficult not to be irritated by these weeds in the flowerbed of life, these mental mosquitoes in the warm evenings of life. But you shouldn't waste your energy and good humour (if you have any) on getting angry over trifles. We have all stamped our foot in annoyance in post office queues that never seem to move forward, or have suffered from high blood pressure thanks to snooty waiters who can't tell the difference between boiled cod and fried pork, and who also add the bill up wrongly (so that the total is too high, never too low). We have all come across unpleasant shop assistants, unfriendly checkout operators and unexpected rain showers when we've left our umbrella at home. Not to mention toothpaste tubes squeezed in the wrong way, delayed trains and cold coffee.

It's not worth getting het up about such things.

The train won't come any sooner, the coffee won't get any warmer and the queue won't start moving any faster if we start frothing at the mouth. Nor is there much point in telling off the unpleasant shop assistant or punching the snooty waiter – that will only lead to unpleasantness.

If we are going to get angry about life's annoyances, we should save our adrenalin for other more important matters. When Her Majesty's Revenue and Customs add our tax bill up wrongly (naturally to their advantage, just like the waiter), and we are forced into a long correspondence to prove that we did not in fact earn twenty-eight-and-a-half million pounds last year, but £28, 500, it's OK to get hot under the collar. Especially as HM Revenue & Customs expect to receive £12 million in unpaid tax immediately, or hefty fines will apply.

We have all come across UNPLEASANT shop assistants, unfriendly checkout operators and UNEXPECTED showers.

When you have been saving up and looking forward to your annual package holiday all year, but when you arrive at your destination (seven hours late) you find that your hotel is only half-built, it's only human and perfectly understandable to be somewhat annoyed. The local courier offers you an attractive alternative hotel, ten miles from the beach. "But I think there is some kind of bus service from the hotel to the beach," the courier informs you, sounding doubtful. Unfortunately you will have to share your room with two unknown alcoholics who couldn't get into the hotel they had ordered either. Your holiday turns out rather differently from what you had planned, and it's not surprising that you get angry.

So it's a matter of distinguishing between petty and major annoyances, and only becoming irritated by the big ones. Mind you, being served with cold coffee is enough to drive you up the wall.

✦

JOBS TO GO FOR

Certain professions stand out as being more attractive
and worth going into than others. It seems to be more
fun being a pop star than an accountant. There is reason
to believe that film stars lead a more glamorous life than
miners. Sometimes, at least. So what jobs should you aim
at in order to achieve an exciting, satisfactory and rich life?
There are many possibilities. Here are a few suggestions.

Pop star
There are many advantages to being a pop star. Not only
do they earn vast amounts of money, but they also lead a
very pleasant life in many other ways. As a pop star you can
dress as you like, without being arrested by the police for
disorderly conduct. You can wander around town in orange
crocodile-skin trousers (uncomfortable but expensive), red
pig-skin shoes and a hat made of dried chanterelles. Nor
will you raise an eyebrow if, as a pop idol, you behave badly
in all kinds of situations. Pop stars are expected to behave
in ways no ordinary mortal would dream of. You will be
admired and written about, and every time you get married,
get divorced or belch, you'll hit the headlines. That can be
good for one's self-esteem. Of course, you must have certain
special qualifications. But you don't need to be able to sing,
which is good to know.

Excavator operator
Operating a mechanical digger is very satisfying. This is
because it is very obvious what you are doing, and what you
have done. When his day's work is finished and it's time to
go home, an excavator operator can survey what he's done
with considerable satisfaction. What used to be a flat piece
of land is now a huge crater. Or where there had been an

enormous pile of sand or gravel there is now nothing. There are few jobs that can show a worker what he has achieved in such an uplifting way. Like a pop star, an excavator operator also works in front of an audience. People love to stop and watch as a mechanical digger chews its way through the earth. Perhaps there are not so many groupies hanging round an excavator operator, but then, as we all know, you can't have everything. And besides, not everybody can get rid of piles so quickly. That's a very useful attribute.

Astronaut
This is a good job to have if you want to get away from it all and see the world.

Friend of the monarchy

This is a splendid if somewhat remarkable job title. Certain people are referred to in all kinds of circumstances as "friends of the monarchy". You don't hear nearly so often references to him or her being a "friend of carpenters", or a "friend of chief executive officers", or a "friend of office cleaners" or a "friend of bailiffs". (Although perhaps it's not all that strange that you never come across one of the latter.)

Being a "friend of the monarchy" sounds like a pleasant sort of life. It's not clear if you need to have another career besides that of friend of the monarchy, or whether being friends with monarchs is a full-time occupation. As the title suggests, being a friend of the monarchy means being a friend of the Queen. That is bound to be enjoyable and is presumably much more fun than being unemployed. All those state banquets, grouse shoots and balls at the Palace! If you're a close friend of the Queen no doubt you'll be able to get some autographed ten pence pieces from her.

Daydreamer

This is a pleasant, attractive occupation that doesn't need too much in the way of qualifications. You don't need any formal training to become a daydreamer, and most universities and colleges don't have Departments of Daydreaming. (Although in some university departments you can often come across a collection of daydreamers, who get together and enjoy daydreaming without learning anything.) As a daydreamer you just dream all day long, and so time goes by without your needing to give it any assistance. Anybody can become a daydreamer, as long as their feet are sufficiently far off the ground.

Celebrity chef

For some unfathomable reason it's very prestigious to be a celebrity chef. Celebrity chefs are admired and lionized. Being able to make a tasty sauce with little bits of chewed-up mushrooms in it is more praiseworthy than being able to conduct a heart operation or build a house. Nobody knows why. Being able to make baked ostrich tail with a dash of angostura, or a whipped lobster with sauce flambé made from small ecologically-grown raspberry drops, is considered to be a heroic feat. As a celebrity chef you will be popular with all walks of life, and everybody will want your recipe for burnt turnips. It's not so difficult to become a celebrity chef, as long as you remember that a fan oven is not the place put your over-enthusiastic admirers while you're busy cooking.

As a celebrity chef you will be POPULAR with all walks of life, and everybody will want your recipe for burnt turnips.

✪

DO-IT-YOURSELF!

"There's only one way to get things done – do them yourself."

"There's only one way of doing things – without delay."

You might think it's easy to object to the two quotations above. You surely don't need to do everything yourself, you can ask somebody else to do things. True, you can: but if you do, it's not at all certain that they will get done. At least, not in the way you had in mind. And probably not before next Thursday (and everything has to be done by Monday at the latest.) Of course things can be done by others, the opening quotations don't need to apply 100% of the time. If we want to send a letter to somebody, it's sufficient to write it ourselves, stick the stamps on the envelope ourselves and take it to the post box ourselves. Usually. There's no need for us to take it to the addressee's front door (especially if he or she lives in Greenland).

A good rule of thumb, however, is to try to do things yourself, because then you know they will be done. (Another certain way of getting things done is to forbid your children to do whatever it is.) But you shouldn't sit and wait for somebody else to do something you really ought to do yourself, because there is a considerable risk that it won't get done at all. Nor is there any point in sitting and waiting for yourself to do it. That can take some time. You should not put off until tomorrow what you have already put off until today. Do it right away. Or at least, immediately after your coffee break. God didn't create urgency, He merely said: "Hurry up!"

✺

HONESTY IS ALL VERY WELL, BUT…

We have to learn to be honest. Honesty lasts longest, according to an old saying, and at an early age we have it drummed into us that it's wrong to tell lies. That's absolutely true, it is wrong to tell lies, but…

What do you think of people who call a spade a spade? People who are always totally honest and say exactly what they think?

"What do you think of my new dress? Pretty, isn't it?"

"No, I don't think so. It's pretty awful. Makes you look even fatter."

There are some plain-speakers who are actually malevolent, and their total candour is an excuse for being malevolent under the guise of honesty.

"But you asked me what I thought!"

There are also plain-speakers who are honest without wanting to be malicious. They are just awkward, tactless or a bit dim. When poor Andy, who has been ill for a long time, says: "I feel much better now, how do you think I look?", the plain speaking nitwit says: "I don't think you look very well at all. You look like Uncle Ken did. He looked almost exactly the same just before he died."

People who call a spade a spade, whether they are driven by malice or stupidity, are people you should avoid talking to or inviting to your home.

"What did you think of the fish stew? It's a recipe I got from my mother."

"It tasted a bit like a dishcloth. Is it supposed to?"

But you can learn something from these plain-speakers, namely that the truth is sometimes a tender flower that has to be handled with care. There are occasions when total honesty is out of place. *There are situations in which kindness and consideration is more important than the honesty we've had drummed into us.* When the truth is hurtful and serves no useful purpose, we should ask ourselves if we should perhaps be a little economical with it. This applies to both everyday trivialities, "do you think my bottom looks big in this?", and in more serious situations. Just like a lot of other things that are good and useful in the right dosage, but harmful in too large portions, honesty can be overdone.

> There are plain-speakers who are ACTUALLY malevolent, and their candour is an excuse for being malevolent.

✸

SAY "AND" INSTEAD OF "BUT"

It's easy to say "but" when you ought to say "and".

Take the following sentence, for instance: "I thought I'd go out for a little walk, but it was raining, so I stayed at home." Now, if we replace the word "but" by "and", we get a completely different sentence: "I thought I'd go out for a little walk and it was raining, so I took my raincoat and umbrella." By substituting "and" for "but", we get out and have a splendid and healthy walk in the refreshing rain.

You can replace "but" by "and" in all kinds of situations, on big occasions and minor ones.

"I thought I'd have a ginger biscuit with my coffee but there weren't any left, so I had to drink my coffee on its own."

This is not an incident of major significance, but even so, it can be changed: "I thought I'd have a ginger biscuit with my coffee and there weren't any left, so I had a custard cream instead. It was very good."

You can also use the recommended change of wording on rather more significant occasions.

"I was thinking of marrying Beryl, but she didn't want to marry me."

Cross out "but" and insert "and" instead, and get yourself a new life: "I was thinking of marrying Beryl and she didn't want to, so I married Beryl's sister instead. We're very happy together. Beryl has emigrated to America and become an alcoholic."

The next time you're about to say "but", ask yourself if it's possible to say "and" instead.

❂

"WHAT IF YOU DIE AND THEN FALL ILL?"

Life is not only a sexually transmitted disease with a 100% mortality rate, it's also a hazardous undertaking. It can go up and it can go down, and you can be exposed to all kinds of unpleasantness. You can be robbed, sacked, run over, lost or struck by rising damp. You can be attacked by fire, burglars, torrential rain or termites. That's why some bright spark came up with the idea of insurance policies. You can insure yourself against anything imaginable, and a lot of things that are unimaginable. All you need to do is pay insurance premiums that go up in leaps and bounds every year. Then if something unpleasant happens to you, your policy is invalid.

In every insurance document, in very small print, there is a clause saying that if something happens, your policy won't cover you for it. If your cellar is flooded, your flood damage insurance isn't valid because the water entered your cellar at an angle. It has to enter in a direct line for your policy to be valid. (Paragraph 18, sub-section 23.) How do you tell whether the water came in a direct line or at an angle? That's for the insurance company to decide.

"Oh, so I'm not entitled to any compensation?"

"No, I'm afraid not. But you can still carry on paying your premiums."

In order to enjoy a better life, avoid meeting people who sell life and accident insurance. It is very depressing to talk to such salesmen. They always start their conversation with the same cheerful question: "What will happen if you die or fall seriously ill?" You glance uneasily at the mirror and ask yourself: "Do I look ill? Why is he asking me that?"

"What will happen to your family if you die or fall seriously ill?" the salesman goes on to ask, spreading good cheer all round. "Have you ever thought what it would be like to be an invalid?"

No, you've never given that a thought. You've got better things to think about than what it would be like to be an invalid. But the insurance salesman doesn't give up that easily. "You could be seriously ill, long-term, and then become an invalid and then die. What do you say to that? Or you might die and then fall ill."

How do you reply to a question like that? The pessimistic insurance salesman then spells out how miserable and painful your life will be if you die and then fall ill. It doesn't sound pleasant. "But," says the insurance salesman solemnly, "this would enable you to do something about it." Really? Can he cure the sick and bring the dead back to life? No, that's not the solution he has in mind for any problems you might have. The answer is to take out an insurance policy with the company he represents. For no more than a small fortune in insurance premiums, you can get comprehensive cover against any eventuality that might befall you. If you were to die, for instance, (in a way approved of by the company), your surviving relatives will receive a large sum of money enabling them to live it up. Now that sounds nice, doesn't it?

You should avoid these depressing insurance agents. It's possible to have a better life and sensible insurance policies without having to listen to their sales pitch of gloom and doom. When they try to sell you a life insurance policy, you can tell them you have no intention of dying. That's almost as good as a the classic story about the insurance salesman who tried to sell a combined fire and theft policy for a motor car. "Combined fire and theft policy?" wondered the car owner. "Why would I want that? Nobody would want to steal a burning car."

✱

JOBS TO AVOID

There are certain careers you should avoid if you want to enjoy a good life. Jobs that for one reason or another can make life sheer hell for whoever has to do them. Here are a few examples of posts you should decline to accept, if you are ever offered them.

Minister for Immigration

For God's sake, don't become Minister for Immigration!

People who don't like immigrants and think we shouldn't accept any will hate you. People who love immigrants and think we should open our borders to all and sundry will hate you. Individuals who are not quite sure what they ought to think about the sensitive immigration question will hate you. Your colleagues, all of them capable, clever and hard-working civil servants, will hate you. The Prime Minister, who will take every opportunity to tell everybody that he has "complete confidence" in you, will hate you. If you have a dog, a faithful, loyal and good-hearted golden retriever, as soon as that dog hears you have been appointed Minister for Immigration, it will hate you. That friendly dog, who has never hurt a fly, will bite your leg and pee on your new carpet the moment you become Minister for Immigration.

Your better half will no longer wish to be seen in your company, and strangely enough, your old friends will always be otherwise engaged whenever you call them to arrange a meeting. "Saturday?" they'll say. "Sorry, I have to be at home then. We're going to make models from chewed bread."

Models from chewed bread? That's not how it used to be before you became Minister for Immigration. But the worst part will be the thrashing you receive from the mass media.

And thrashed you will be.

You'll be thrashed, whipped, racked, keel-hauled and flogged by the mass media. The newspapers will write about little Pedro, aged six, who's going to be sent back to where he came from. Little Pedro is an orphan, depressed, allergic, asthmatic, poor, and he's lost his front teeth. His life story would wring tears out of a stone. No human being has ever suffered as much misery as poor little Pedro. His only friend is a little three-legged dog, but of course, he won't be able to take the dog with him when he's deported. Little Pedro has sad, brown eyes, as big as saucers. And whose fault is it that Pedro is going to be expelled? Well of course, it's the Minister for Immigration.

You'll be interviewed on the television by reporters who attack you like a pack of starving wolves. How can you possibly deport this innocent little child?! How could anybody make such a brutal, heartless decision? Don't you realise that Pedro has a cough and his little dog has a limp?! Besides, there's a rumour that his dog also has a cough. This is a scandal, and the mass media demand your head on a plate.

Whatever you do, don't become Minister for Immigration!

Racing cyclist

What does a racing cyclist do all day long?

He rides a bike.

He rides, rides, rides. If it's not a race, it's practice. Day in, day out, he sits on his bike and pedals away, pedals away. From morning till night, pedalling away. Pedalling away. Can you imagine a better symbol for a life that's as boring and monotonous and miserable as it's possible to be? No matter how you pedal, you're always going uphill or into a head wind. Turning round won't make any difference, because the winds and the hills will do the same.

If you're unlucky, you'll be good enough to enter the Tour de France. Have you any idea how big France is? And France is not especially flat. On the contrary. And at regular intervals you'll fall off and be accused of taking drugs.

Being a racing cyclist must be one of the most boring jobs in the world. All that pedalling — where does it get you? From nowhere to nowhere, just like life when it's at its most boring. But life ought not to be boring, it ought to be pleasant. Don't become a racing cyclist.

Secondary school teacher for the CG stream
CG stands for Criminal Gangster, and it's not an easy stream for teachers to teach. Most of the pupils in this stream have already passed through the AG stream lower down the school (AG = Apprentice Gangster), and many of them took Destruction and Vandalism as their special subjects. Several of the boys started taking anabolic steroids while they were still at primary school, and by the time they get to the sixth form they look like Arnold Schwarzenegger's big brother. They are muscular and strong, and they like to take part in the sports that are only available to the CG stream: Crashing Cars, Punching Policemen and Throwing the Teacher.

As a CG-stream teacher, you are exposed every day of the week to stress, threats and unpleasantness. It doesn't matter what your special subject is, the CG pupils will have no interest at all in anything you say. They much prefer knife-throwing or practising karate kicks on living targets. Research has shown that the survival rate for teachers of CG-stream pupils is roughly the same as that for soldiers in the first wave of the Normandy landings on D-Day. One has to conclude that being a teacher for the CG stream is not a career to be recommended.

Lion tamer

One of these days the lions will get fed up of your waving a chair and a whip at them. They'll say to each other: "Why on earth should we keep playing along with this nonsense? It's undignified."

"You're absolutely right. Let's pack it in. Besides, I feel a bit on the hungry side, I think."

"Funny you should say that. So do I. He looks as though he's got nice buttocks."

"Yes. Shall we…?"

"Why not? Are we all ready for a little snack?"

"Yes, yes!"

The next day you'll be far more famous than you ever were when you were alive.